D1593283

Femininity as Alienation

Ann Foreman

Femininity as Alienation
Women and the Family in Marxism and Psychoanalysis

Pluto Press

First published 1977 by Pluto Press Limited,
Unit 10 Spencer Court, 7 Chalcot Road, London NW1 8LH
Copyright © Pluto Press 1977
ISBN 0 904383 62 8 paperback
     0 904383 63 6 hardback
Cover design by Richard Hollis, GrR
Printed in Great Britain by
The Camelot Press Limited, Southampton

Contents

to my parents

Preface

For over a decade now the shifting roles of men and women have been a matter of controversy. Not everyone has posed the problem in terms of the oppression of women, but frequently use of the term 'the permissive society' in such discussions indicates that there is an underlying questioning of sexual norms. But while writers from the women's movement, both in Britain and internationally, have provided some of the best descriptive accounts of the relations between men and women very little has yet been produced in terms of analysis. And though descriptive accounts give women in the women's movement strength in the knowledge that their individual experiences have wider social significance they are not the material out of which a political perspective can be constructed.

Those writers who have taken an analytic approach to women's oppression have tended to concentrate on two apparently separate areas of concern — either on what has been termed 'the political economy of domestic labour' or on the problem of sexuality. The first has drawn heavily on marxism while the second has used Freudian psychoanalysis as its reference point. Indeed it appears that research in these areas is developing along parallel lines. But this divided approach to women's oppression is not something restricted to recent times. Looking back into the history of the marxist movement I found that the separation of sexuality from economics has been a recurring theme. With this discovery came the realisation that the problem of developing a theory of women's oppression was not one of adding to the existing body of socialist and marxist thought, as it is usually presented, but questioning its whole tradition. Given this it seemed possible that the questions that writers such as Georg Lukacs and Jean-Paul Sartre had posed for marxism might have a relevance in this context. Gradually it became apparent that the abstract problem of individual action raised in their work had a definite connection to a theory of the relations between men and women. This book, then, is the result of developing those connections.

1.

Feminism and the limits of liberalism

You speak, Mr Asquith, the suffragist said,
of the will of the people wholesale;
but has the idea never entered your head
that the people are not wholly male?[1]

Women's oppression has only relatively recently become a political issue. The first serious debate on it took place in Europe in the last century following the French Revolution.

In Britain Mary Wollstonecraft started that debate with the publication of her treatise *A Vindication of the Rights of Women* in 1790. In it she challenged the idea that human rights and freedom applied only to men. Radical thought at that time was founded on the belief that man was a rational animal and that society, if it were based on this human capacity, could be both free and happy. Using these basic ideas as her starting point Mary Wollstonecraft argued to her audience that the oppression of women was inconsistent with them.

Consider – I address you as a legislator – whether, when men contend for their freedom and to be allowed to judge for themselves respecting their own happiness, it be not inconsistent and unjust to subjugate women, even though you firmly believe that you are acting in the manner best calculated to promote happiness? Who made man the exclusive judge, if women must partake with him of the gift of reason?[2]

But while she made the abstract case for women's liberation, her only strategy to achieve it was her appeal to reason. However, without any significant social movement to back up that appeal, and with the case against women resting on centuries of tradition, the likelihood of its realisation was negligible.

Later on in the nineteenth century John Stuart Mill, with rather less vivacity, returned to the main themes of Mary Wollstonecraft's argument in his essay *The Subjection of Women* (1869). He considered that the oppression of women was the one thing that halted mankind's triumphant march to a free society.

> The social subordination of women thus stands out as an isolated fact in modern social institutions; a solitary breach of what has become their fundamental law; a single relic of an old world of thought and practice exploded in everything else but retained in the one thing of universal interest.[3]

But while John Stuart Mill fought for political rights for women, particularly over the question of suffrage, he did not believe that their attainment would decisively alter the whole range of relations between men and women. For he maintained that the private relations between husband and wife would remain the same.

> When the support of the family depends, not on property, but on earnings, the common arrangement, by which the man earns the income and the wife superintends the domestic expenditure, seems to me in general the most suitable division of labour between the two persons. . . . In an otherwise just state of things, it is not, therefore, I think, a desirable custom that the wife should contribute by her labour to the income of the family. . . . Like a man when he chooses a profession, so, when a woman marries, it may be understood that she makes a choice of the management of a household, and the bringing up of a family, as the call upon her exertions, during as many years of her life as she may be required for the purpose; and that she renounces, not all other objects and occupations, but all which are not consistent with the requirements of this.[4]

John Stuart Mill's conservatism on this point covered a dilemma which had prevented radical thought in general from espousing the cause of women during the course of the nineteenth century. Indeed many radicals had not only been hesitant on the issue but often downright hostile – a position expressed vividly by a pamphlet distributed during the French Revolution.

> Civil and political liberty is of no use to women and should therefore be kept from them. Since they are destined to spend their entire lives either under their fathers' or husbands' protection, and are born to be dependent from the cradle to the grave they have been endowed only with private virtues. . . . A woman is acceptable only in the context of her father's or husband's household. She needs to know nothing of what goes on outside beyond what they may see fit to tell her.[5]

Liberal thought, which provided the political framework for radicals in the nineteenth century, assumed that the realm of freedom was in the individual's private life, within the family. If men exercised their will freely in the public sphere they would collide with each other's interests. Accordingly the state should have the power to regulate their activities in this sphere in order to secure the unrestrained exercise of their freedom within the private sphere of the family. It was this separation of public life from the family and the restriction of women to the latter which gave the freedom of the individual man its meaning. Women as the embodiment of the man's freedom were themselves above it. This point is illustrated by the stand taken by William Gladstone, leader of the Liberal Party, when he described women's suffrage as,

> one of those questions which it would be intolerable to mix up with purely political and Party debate. If there be a subject in the whole compass of human life and experience that is sacred, beyond all other subjects, it is the character and position of women.[6]

In short to campaign for the vote or, worse, for a fundamental change in the nature of the relations between men and women was to undermine the very foundations of liberal freedom.

In the twentieth century radical thought has been dominated by the ideas of Karl Marx and Sigmund Freud. Through their major theories of ideology and the unconscious respectively, they struck a blow at the liberal belief that change could be obtained by appeals to men's rationality.

Marx, in his analysis of the class antagonisms of society, argued that rational persuasion was useless in reconciling the basic differences between the interests of the working class and the bourgeoisie. Only the revolutionary action of the working class, based on an understanding of those differences, could shift the hold of ideology which arose from the domination of one class by another.

Freud, on the other hand, by means of his analysis of the structuring of the individual's mind into a conscious and unconscious area, threw doubt on the very existence of men's rationality and with it on the liberal trust in the progressive improvement of society. At the same time, in his study of the sexual lives of men and women, he drew attention to this aspect of the range of relations between them and so initiated the political questioning of their 'natural' pattern.

While both Marx and Freud referred to the question of women's oppression in their writings neither made it a major concern: nevertheless, their contribution to its theorisation was crucial. For more important than what they failed to say, although this in itself was interesting, was the fact they enabled the development of an alternative theoretical and political framework to that of liberalism in which the question could be posed afresh.

2.

Freud: the importance of sexuality

Before Freud the term sexuality was infrequently used. When it was it was limited to the question of reproduction, and usually the reproduction of animals and plants. Freud changed all that. Firstly he extended the concept of sexuality 'far enough to be able to comprise the sexual life of perverts and children'.[1] And secondly he elevated it to a position of central importance in the structuring of all social behaviour, not only its overt sexual forms.

In this respect Freud's *Three Essays on the Theory of Sexuality* (1905) is a classic. In it he announced the discovery of infantile sexuality. This discovery is important in a number of different ways. For a start, it breaks through the reduction of sexuality to reproductive genital sexuality. The sexual life of children shows how sexuality can be 'polymorphous', that is it can be located in areas other than the genitals; for example the anus or even the thumb. It also shows that it does not have to be directed towards another person but can be 'auto-erotic'. As well as recognising children's sexual attitudes Freud introduced the idea of 'infantile amnesia'. This not only pre-empted the horror that his ideas created but suggested that there was something blocking each individual's memory of his or her own childhood sexual experiences, and so pointed to his theories of the unconscious.

With this work, then, Freud drew a new line between normal and abnormal sexuality. Previously that line had been firmly drawn on the basis of moral criteria; sexual perversion was a sin against God and man. But Freud considered that sexuality developed through a number of, in a sense, perverted stages before it attained its normal heterosexual form. The first two stages Freud termed the oral and the anal respectively. Oral sexuality naturally arises from the pleasure the child receives from suckling the mother's breast and which can be transferred to substitutes like its own thumb. Anal sexuality develops with the enjoyment the child receives from controlling the expulsion of faecal matter. Freud denoted the establishment of the mouth and anus as erotogenic zones, the connection of these areas to vital somatic functions, and the fact that the child can obtain sexual pleasure from them without the intrusion of an external object, as essential characteristics of infantile sexuality. The third phallic stage laid the ground for the castration and Oedipus complexes which Freud was to explain in detail at a later date. With the resolution of these complexes the child went into a period of latency when all sexual activity apparently ceased. Following this, the normal individual emerged as an adult with a heterosexual and genitally based sexual outlook.

However, the path to normal sexuality does not run as smoothly as it has been described here. The resignation of the child's polymorphous sexual enjoyment does not occur without pain and difficulty. And indeed, it was largely to explain why the child abandoned this enjoyment in favour of genital and reproductive sexuality that Freud put forward the complementary concepts of the Oedipus and castration complexes.

With the analysis of these complexes Freud moved into stormy waters in regard to the question of female sexuality. Feminists have accused him of developing his analysis on the basis of the male child's experience alone and therefore of its being inappropriate to describe the situation of women.[2] And it is true that Freud only fully theorised its application to women at a relatively late date in his articles 'Female Sexuality' (1931) and 'Femininity' (1933). This is not, however, the most serious criticism.

Briefly, the Oedipus complex is the child's desire to kill the father and have sexual intercourse with the mother. With the boy child the process takes place in the following way. The boy regards the father as a rival in his love for the mother and would like to kill him. But he also fears him. This fear springs from the belief that his father is likely to castrate him. This belief in turn is founded on the revelation, either from seeing his mother or perhaps a sister naked, that there are creatures without penises who have presumably been castrated. And in the end the boy's fear of his father wins over his desire for the mother and so he enters the period of latency.

With the girl child it is the specific relation between the Oedipus and castration complexes that determines her differing path to female sexuality. Like the boy the girl's first love object is her mother. This immediately gives a different twist to the girl's pattern of development. The boy's first object of desire as well as his later ones as an adult are female. The girl, however, must change from desiring a female to desiring a male. Freud describes the process in the following way. When the girl sees the genitals of the opposite sex, she is struck by the penis's superior quality over her clitoris. Up to this point in the phallic stage the clitoris had been the focal point of the girl's sexual activity. Freud terms this active desire of the girl for her mother based on the clitoris 'masculine'. But in recognising the inferiority of her clitoris the girl turns away from her mother in anger and wishes above all else for a penis herself. She is angry with her mother who is responsible for her deficiency and who is unworthy of her desire by the fact that she too is without a penis. The girl now turns to her father with the hope that he can make good her lack. At the same time she drops the phallic sexuality of the clitoris in favour of the passive vagina, which Freud considered the true seat of female genital sexuality. The girl's wish for a penis is replaced with its symbolic equivalent, the wish for a baby. And in time the girl substitutes the desire for other men in place of that for her father.

From this analysis of the resolution of the Oedipus complex in boys and girls we get the rather depressing picture of male sexuality equated with activity and female with passivity. Freud, however, and feminists[3] who have been sympathetic to his ideas, have hastened to modify it. In particular they have pointed to his concept of bisexuality.

> Both men and women are bisexual in the psychological sense; I shall conclude that you have decided in your own minds to make 'active' coincide with 'masculine' and 'passive' with 'feminine'. But I advise you against it.[4]

But does this concept of bisexuality make Freud a sexual liberationist, as some have gone on to suggest? While this concept allowed Freud to analyse homosexuality or lesbianism as a possible and relatively frequent outcome of a fixated sexual development it did not make his criteria for normal adult sexuality any less rigid. And Freud did not consider this criterion as culture bound, and therefore susceptible to change, but believed that it under-pinned all cultural norms.

To explain, let us return to the castration complex in the sexual development of boys and girls. In both cases, in the girl's in the form of penis envy, its onset begins a crucial period. To use Freud's own words: 'The discovery that she is castrated is a turning-point in a girl's growth.'[5]

But this discovery, and therefore ultimately the complex itself, is dependent on the girl and the boy seeing the genitals of each other's sex. In other words, the development of female and male sexuality is conditioned by the anatomical differences between the sexes. And as we have seen in the case of the woman this means sexual passivity and the wish for a child. So, for Freud, as a product of biology this process, penis-envy-passivity-wish-for-a-child, is ahistorical. Ironically the concept of bisexuality represents a sense of conservatism in Freud. For it represents an inability to maintain a belief in any form of interpersonal sexuality that cannot be traced back, even in a secondary way, to a male-female relationship. Why otherwise was the active period of the girl's sexual growth termed 'masculine'? The answer is that as the girl's love-object was female her aggressiveness had to be male, and it was this which provoked Freud into postulating the new category of 'psychological

FREUD: THE IMPORTANCE OF SEXUALITY 17

bisexuality'. Freud's admonishments to his audience on the use of the terms masculinity-activity, feminity-passivity are in bad faith, given his own inability to break out of that framework.

While the concept of bisexuality has been detached from its context within Freud's system to emphasise the revolutionary implications of psychoanalysis,[6] there are those who have stressed its conservative and even reactionary overtones. Marie Bonaparte, whose work was viewed favourably by Freud, did precisely this. She used Freud's view that psychological bisexuality is more prominent in women to develop the thesis that the male sex is progressive while the female sex is regressive. As she wrote:

> only the male will attain the full somatic development possible to the race. . . . The general development of women, however, will come to a stop at puberty through the maturation of the organs destined for maternity; functions which absorb a large part of the energy which is used by the male in building up his whole orgasm. It would appear, therefore, that whereas the male usually passes through an intersexual crisis of the feminoid type, before full puberty is reached, and before virility is fully established, the female will experience the customary intersexual crisis of a viriloid type after the menopause, when the inhibitory influence of the ovaries disappears.[7]

From this she deduces for normal female sexuality an even more sharply delineated path than Freud's. Marie Bonaparte considered that there were three types of woman.

> The first type soon succeed in substituting the desire for the penis for that of a child, and become true women; normal vaginal, maternal. The next abandon all competition with men feeling themselves too unequal, renounce all hope of obtaining an external love object and, socially and psychically, achieve a status among humans like that of the workers we see in the anthill or hive. Lastly, there are those who deny reality and never accept it; these cling desperately to the psychical and organic male elements in all women: the masculinity complex and the clitoris.[8]

While Freud was never as crude as this, the example of Marie Bonaparte shows how the ambiguities in his writing as to the level of biological determinism he was suggesting could be refracted through the later works of psychoanalysis.

At the beginning we referred to the new line that Freud drew between normal and abnormal sexuality. We are now in a position to establish what the distinction was that Freud made. Although Freud's line of divide was not based crudely on what was moral and what was sinful, it was nevertheless drawn just as firmly. For Freud the sexual framework of the individual and of society at large was hierarchical. In a normally organised person or in a relatively harmonious society, it took the form of a pyramid. Genital reproductive sexuality was at the top and all other forms of sexuality took part in founding and maintaining it. So while Freud avoided the heavy moral overtones of previous sexual theorists he did not make his actual criterion for normal sexuality less rigid. Indeed, while the reasoning behind it was very different, he shared with them the belief that if society was to survive then perverse forms of sexuality had to be repressed in favour of genital reproductive sexuality.

We have looked at the Oedipus complex from the point of view of it being the dynamic in the child's development from polymorphous infantile sexuality to adult genital sexuality. But we have still left some questions unanswered. Why did Freud think that the sight of 'castrated' genitals should have such an effect on the child? And why did Freud insist that the Oedipus complex explained cultural norms and not the other way around? Freud discusses these questions in his book *Totem and Taboo* (1913).

There he puts forward the idea that the first human group was established as the enforced rule of one male individual over all individuals. This 'father' monopolised all the women and subjugated all the 'sons' to his power. The 'sons' became more and more jealous of their 'father' and angry at his powerful position until their hatred brought them together. In league they overthrew him, killed him and devoured his body. According to Freud it was this original act of killing the father that 'was the beginning of so many things – of social organisation, of moral restrictions and of religion'.[9]

This first enactment of the Oedipal situation laid the basis for all social activity. Previous to it there had been no form of communal life, each individual acted alone and against the other. So important was the act that its original perpetrators deified the father and the memory of the act has been rehearsed through the Oedipus complex in the lives of each generation since then. And so its resolution stands as the prerequisite for the entrance of each individual into adult social life, while the fear of every child of castration symbolises the murder of the ancestral father.

In *Totem and Taboo* Freud was at pains to make clear that this explanation of the origins of society only had the status of a hypothesis. Nevertheless in all his major works on social psychology, such as *Group Psychology and the Analysis of the Ego* (1921), *Civilization and Its Discontents* (1929) and *Moses and Monotheism* (1939) he worked it into their central themes. In fact, whether or not Freud maintained it was a hypothesis is largely irrelevant. For in developing his theories around it, Freud committed himself to its assumptions.

What, then, are the assumptions of *Totem and Taboo*? To begin with it assumed that the first social formations were patriarchal. This assumption in turn led Freud to make two further ones: firstly, that the relations between men and women from the very beginning took an active/passive form – men dominated women – and secondly, that fatherhood was the primary social institution.

While it is unlikely that we will ever know what the exact nature of the first human societies was, an argument in favour of their having been matrilineal seems equally as convincing as Freud's. Such an argument, moreover, has the merit of not assuming without explanation the dominance of one sex over the other. Evelyn Reed in her recent book *Women's Evolution* puts forward just such a hypothesis. She suggests that the first sexual relations that took place within a recognisably human society were not of a permanent nature. However, when such relations did begin to take on more permanence it was the man who visited the woman's clan. These semi-permanent forms of relations, she considers, pre-date the more permanent monogamous ones of patriarchal societies.

Without more evidence Evelyn Reed's argument remains unproved. Evidence can be brought to bear, however, on the related assumption of Freud, that fatherhood was the primary social institution. This assumption was, if we remember, central not only to the myth of *Totem and Taboo* but also to Freud's claim for the universal applicability of the Oedipus complex. For Freud used the Oedipal situation to explain the processes by which the first social relations were established and by which each individual of each subsequent generation took his or her place within society. In both the father was the primal figure. There is, however, anthropological evidence to suggest that fatherhood is a social invention and not an essential precondition for a society to come about.

While disagreeing on most other major issues such diverse writers as Evelyn Reed, Margaret Mead, Ann Oakley and Claude Lévi-Strauss all agree on this. Evelyn Reed points out that primitive people did not know the facts about the birth process or even that sexual intercourse between a man and a woman is an indispensable first step in conception. Consequently, the role of the man in the process was frequently denied and in such societies there was no idea of paternity. She records that in many parts of Australia, New Guinea, New Caledonia and Central Borneo this was the case until quite recent times.[10] Margaret Mead refers to the present Tobrianders as 'conspicuous for their denial of the father's bio-logical role in procreation'.[11] Since the concept of paternity is re-ported absent from so many societies it is difficult to maintain that it could be a pre-condition for initial social relations. Moreover, it follows that the concept of fatherhood cannot be based upon it, but must have evolved in some other way. Evelyn Reed argues that fatherhood as a social institution arose out of a set of maternal functions performed by the man for his wife's child.[12]

The idea that fatherhood is located in a series of functions rather than in biology is substantiated both by Ann Oakley and Claude Lévi-Strauss. Ann Oakley describes the homosexual marriages of the Mohave Indians both between biological females and biological males.

> 'Male wives' feigned menstruation by cutting their thighs monthly, faked pregnancy, stuffing rags to the shape of a pregnant womb, and imitated labour. Female 'husbands' were socially recognised to be the fathers of their wives' children.[13]

Claude Lévi-Strauss notes that in several parts of Africa, women of high rank were allowed to marry other women and have them bear children through the services of unacknowledged male lovers. The noble women were entitled to become 'father' of their children and to transmit to them their own name, status and wealth.[14]

It seems, in contradiction to Freud, that in a substantial number of cultures the figure of the mother rather than the father is the central figure in myth and ceremony. Margaret Mead investigated a number of societies where womb-envying rather than penis-envying patterns are more appropriate to describe their cultural values. She gives an account of male initiatory rites in the Pacific Islands in these terms:

> Sometimes more overtly, sometimes less, these imitations of birth go on, as the initiates are swallowed by the crocodile that represents the male group and come out new born at the other end; as they are housed in wombs, or fed on blood, fattened, hand-fed, and tended by male 'mothers'. Behind the cult lies the myth that in some way all of this was stolen from the women; sometimes they were killed to get it.[15]

The study of anthropology also sheds a new light on the relation of the Oedipus complex to the question of incest taboo.

Freud believed that the existence of incest taboos in all known cultures was a testimony to the strength and universal relevance of the Oedipus complex. According to the dictionary definition incest is, 'sexual intercourse between those who are closely related by blood kinship'.[16] Evelyn Reed points out that in many tribal societies the taboo operated against sexual intercourse between not simply men and women of the same family or clan, but whole phratry that is between individuals who can hardly be considered closely related. From this she suggests that this form of sexual prohibition, although frequently classed as a taboo is quite different and specific to patriarchal societies. The confusion occurred when anthropologists, discovering sexual prohibition in primitive societies, interpreted the information through the only form of prohibition with which they were familiar, namely that of incest. J.Goody in his article 'Incest and Adultery'[17] backs up this interpretation by outlining the major differences in the system of sexual prohibition in matrilineal and patriarchal societies. In the first the chief sin is sexual intercourse within the clan while in the second it is sexual intercourse with the wife of a kinsman.

Finally, anthropology calls attention to a simple but revealing factor. Freud's insistence on the discovery of the missing penis in the establishment of adult male and female sexuality appears a little ridiculous given the realities of so many societies where nakedness is the rule.

This catalogue of evidence – the establishment of paternity and fatherhood as functions which post-date social organisation; mythologies and sexual prohibitions; and even the absence of clothing in certain societies – shakes the foundations of the Oedipus complex. It cannot be, as Freud had argued, the motif that structures the mind of each individual and shapes each culture. If it does have a relevance it must be of a more limited kind. This shaking of the Oedipus complex from its pride of position in all culture at all times in turn reverberates through Freud's notions of adult male and female sexuality. If we remember, while Freud was willing to include a diversity, and even perversity, of sexual forms within his sexual aetiology his actual criteria for normal genital sexuality remained rigid. But if the Oedipus complex is in some way bound within history and culture it is likely that Freud's norms of sexuality are similarly affected.

However, it is not simply a question of adjusting Freud's ideas and making them apply to a specific time and place. Freud's theories pivot around a certain concept of the individual, of human nature. Remove that and their cohesion is lost, and we are no longer dealing with Freudian psychoanalysis.

Totem and Taboo assumes not only the universal relevance of the patriarchal Oedipus complex but also that aggression is a basic element of human nature. It is no accident that Freud postulated that human history began with an act of murder. Murder and the domination of men over women was the raw material out of which society was constructed. Freud maintained this view of mankind throughout his writings on social themes. In *Civilization and Its Discontents* he characterised man as 'homo homini lupus' – man is a wolf to man. Steadily he built up a picture of society made up of isolated, and in many ways anti-social, individuals. And in his later works[18] he developed his theory of the instincts by suggesting the existence of a death instinct as a way of explaining the prevalence of aggression in all forms of human activity.

Freud's idea of man as isolated and aggressive has its roots in political theory. From Hobbes onwards, political theorists had viewed society as something constructed to safeguard each individual against the aggressive impulses of others. For them, the isolated individual pre-dated the development of social relations. Given this framework the problem to which political theorists continually returned was that of the origins of society. That is, in starting with the existence of the isolated, aggressive individual they then had to suggest a mechanism by which this individual forfeited his unlimited freedom in favour of the constraints of organised society. The concept of the social contract was the most popular solution to this problem. According to this, at some specific time each individual agreed to subsume his will in the general will, represented by organised society or the state. In return for this restriction of his freedom each individual was guaranteed a peaceful life protected from the aggression of others. Hobbes's *Leviathan* originally set this theory of a social contract within a conservative mould but with the writings of Locke and Rousseau it became the reference point for liberal and radical thought.

Although Freud declared himself to be ignorant of political theory his basic sympathies were towards a liberal rather than a conservative outlook. His emphasis on the critical explanation of human action cut across the principles of conservatism – the unquestioning belief in tradition and prejudice. However, while sharing many of the traditional liberal themes, Freud wore his liberalism with a difference.

The social contract was transformed by Freudian psycho-analysis into the murder of the father. And instead of this original social act representing the birth of man's reason, as it did in the liberal model, within Freud's system as the first enactment of the Oedipal situation it stood as a testimony to the forces of man's unconscious mind. But like traditional liberalism Freud saw society as a struggle between rationalism and irrationalism, a struggle between the reason of the individual and the unreason of the crowd.[19] The difference was that Freud was less optimistic about the outcome.

In summary then, from studying Freud's work on social themes a number of points emerge. Firstly, that Freudian psycho-analysis is a coherent system of thought. Freud's understanding of human nature and society are the central concepts around which he developed his theory. This means that any attempt to adopt the ideas of psychoanalysis has to confront this fact. And secondly, it seems that they are indications that while Freud established in psychoanalysis a new area of study, its themes have a definite, if peculiar, relation to the tradition of liberal thought.

3.

Marxism and the origins of women's oppression

The achievement of Freudian psychoanalysis that secured its impact on modern thought was to relate the question of sexuality to social and political theory. Before Freud the sexual life of men and women was not considered to be the subject of analysis. If it was discussed at all it was from the point of view of morality. Freud made it possible for the first time to raise the question of the political implications of sexual relations.

But while Freud made this possible he himself considered it unlikely that there could be political change in this sphere. By ascribing certain essential characteristics to human beings, such as aggression, he ruled out a project of radical change in social relations. And in particular, in attaching such importance to the Oedipus complex Freud denied the possibility of a qualitative change in the relations between men and women. For firstly, as we have seen, the Oedipus complex assumed as its starting point a relation of domination between men and women. And secondly, the resolution of the Oedipus complex in women, Freud considered, established the desire for a baby as the immutable core of femininity.

Marxism developed in opposition to all theories that ascribed such fixity to human beings. Marx argued that the human species creates itself through its productive activity. Through labour human beings change the world they are acting within and continually change the nature of their existence. Men and women work to satisfy their needs but in doing so they create new needs.

Consequently there can be nothing fixed about them. The origins of human society and the distinction between human activity and that of animals lay in the development of humans as conscious beings. Animals are their activity while human beings can distance themselves from their actions and plan their work. But knowledge is a social acquisition; when men and women planned to meet their needs they did it together. As Marx explains:

> Activity and mind, both in their content and in their *mode of existence*, are *social*: *social* activity and *social* mind. The *human* essence of nature first exists only for *social* man; for only here does nature exist for him as a *bond* with *man* — as his existence for the other and the other's existence for him as the life-element of human reality.[1]

For Marx it was therefore a contradiction in terms to consider human beings as pre- or anti-social. He believed that while Freud's egoistic individual did exist within human history, those character-istics arose in a specific set of circumstances and were not essential to mankind.

The major work of classical marxism which analyses the relation between the sexes was written by Engels and not Marx. *The Origin of the Family, Private Property and the State* (1884) attacked the assumption that the patriarchal family was the first form in the relations between the sexes and that it had not been subject to any real historical change. Engels divided the history of human society into three main epochs: savagery, barbarism and civilisation. Each epoch was distinguished by a development in the method of industry and each change in industrial method was accompanied by a change in the relations between the sexes. The 'group marriage' accompanied savagery, the 'pairing marriage' barbarism, and the dawn of civilisation was crowned by the creation of the monogamous family. With civilisation a matrilineal organisation of society, or as Engels termed it, 'mother right', was replaced by a patriarchal one where inheritance was traced through the male. Engels called this 'the world historic defeat of the female sex'.[2] This then is the crucial turning point in the history of the relation between men and women.

However, in his analysis of the period Engels left a residue of ambiguity. He described the process in the following way. With the development of the domestication of animals a source of wealth was established, a surplus over and above what was required for mere subsistence. This production of a surplus provided the man, who was in charge of the herds, with the impetus to establish inheritance through his sons and so to demand a guarantee of the woman's chastity. Gradually the relation between the woman, the man and the children developed into the recognisable form of the patriarchal family. Although there are gaps in the argument – for example one might want explicitly to question why men were originally in charge of the herds – Engels's account seems a reasonable one. In it he had made the innovation in political theory of arguing that a change in the form of industry coincided with a change in the whole mode of human existence, including the most intimate form of relation between men and women. It stood as a concrete application of the marxist thesis that the way human beings produce in society conditions their lives.

Engels, however, offers another account of the process which is not completely in keeping with the first.

> The more the old traditional sexual relations lost their naive, primitive jungle character, as a result of the development of the economic conditions of life, that is, with the undermining of the old communism and the growing density of the population, the more degrading and oppressive must they have appeared to women: the more fervently must they have longed for the right to chastity, to temporary or permanent marriage with one man only, as a deliverance. This advance could not have originated from the men, if only for the reason that they have never – not even to the present day – dreamed of renouncing the pleasures of actual group marriage.[3]

Not only is this incompatible with Engels's original account, but it is also profoundly unmarxist in that it projects on to men and women, essential characteristics, a fixed sexuality unaltered by changes in the social relations. Women view sexual relations as a burden while men are sexually avaricious. This indeed was a continuous theme of *The Origin of the Family, Private Property and the State*. While it is clear that Engels had overlaid his theories with an interpretation of the moral and sexual code of the day, its implications for marxism are serious. The question of men and women's sexuality was thereby detached from marxist economic and historical analysis. Engels illustrated this with his timeless predictions: 'Since sex love is by its very nature exclusive – although this exclusiveness is fully realised today only in the woman – then marriage based on sex love is by its very nature monogamy.'[4]

Engels's lack of precision over the relation of economic and sexual categories also severely damages his analysis of the period of capitalist commodity production.

> Sex love [he wrote] in the relation of husband and wife can only become the rule among the oppressed classes, that is at the present day, among the proletariat, no matter whether this relationship is officially sanctioned or not. . . . Here, there is a complete absence of all property, for the safeguarding and inheritance of which monogamy and male domination were established. Therefore, there is no stimulus whatever here to assert male domination.[5]

Here he has argued that the only economic basis for women's oppression lies in property. Since the proletariat is without property, it also lacks the impetus for male domination. This is not simply an aberration on Engels's part; elsewhere Marx, too, makes a similar point that among the proletariat 'the concept of the family does not exist at all'.[6]

But while all property relations are economic relations, not all economic relations are reducible to those of property. Neither Marx nor Engels analysed the possibility of there being a dynamic for male domination within the working class family other than that of property. Consequently, the marxist analysis of the position of women within the present epoch of capitalism is weak. *The Origin of the Family* left later marxists with the idea that the issue of women's oppression did not pose a particular problem for the class struggle. For if the development of capitalist enterprise was turning women's domestic work into an industry, as Engels had assumed, then women's concerns would become no different from those of the working class as a whole. Any remaining areas of specific concern to women could be taken care of by bourgeois democratic demands – such as the vote. Thus the struggle for women's liberation was reduced to two separate components – the pressing of democratic demands within the framework of capitalism, a strategy rather like that of Mary Wollstonecraft and John Stuart Mill; and the fight for the victory of the proletarian revolution. In fact Engels had prepared the ground for this conclusion in an early, rather enigmatic statement in *The Origin of the Family* on the relation of class oppression to women's oppression:

> The first class antagonism which appears in history coincides with the development of the antagonism between man and woman in monogamian marriage, and the first class oppression with that of the female sex by the male.[7]

The use of the term class, here, in relation to women is out of keeping with its normal application by marxists. And its loose use here adds to the reasons for suspecting the clarity of Engels's analysis in the rest of the work. For by terming women a class Engels conflated the categories of class and sex and thus falsely removed by a sleight of hand the necessity of making a specific analysis of the relation between the two.

4.

The degeneration of the marxist tradition

But what were the practical implications of Marx and Engels's theory of women's oppression? How would the growing working class movement, and in particular those sections of it which adhered to marxism, translate the theory into a developed strategy on this question?

In the International Working Men's Association – the First International – which Marx and Engels helped to set up, the issue raised major dissension. On the two most important questions of the day, that of suffrage and the right of women to work, the movement was split. But while Marx had shown himself to be determined and decisive on other contentious questions, as for example over Proudhon's ideas, his intervention on these ones left much to be desired. His criticisms of the Gotha programme illustrate this well.

This programme, drafted in 1875, was for adoption by the new, unified German Social Democratic Party (SPD) at its founding conference. The SPD was of particular importance since it grew rapidly to be the largest party in Europe to base itself on Marx's ideas, and was taken as a model of what a revolutionary socialist party should be like. The debates and positions which originated in the SPD were later echoed in almost all the European working class organisations. Marx's extensive notes on the draft programme, made from a distance in London, are therefore of great interest. The programme provoked a vigorous debate at the conference, including on the demands relating to women. But while

Marx's remarks on the other major issues had been crucial in clarifying the debate, the ones he made on the question of women were of an entirely different order. It was August Bebel, one of the leading members of the SPD, not Marx, who fought for the conference to adopt a clear position on the emancipation of women. He argued that where the draft document had only referred to adult male suffrage an amendment should be made demanding 'the right to vote for citizens of both sexes'. But the majority opposed it and Bebel's proposal was defeated. Finally, the unity of the party was put above its clarity and an ambiguous formula was adopted which called for 'the right to vote for all citizens', which had the merit of being open to the interpretation of either side of the party.

What then was Marx's contribution to the debate? He concentrated his remarks on the draft programme to the demand for the restriction of female labour. It is worth quoting in full the points he made:

> The standardisation of the working day must include the restriction of female labour, insofar as it relates to the duration, intermissions, etc., of the working day; otherwise it could only mean the exclusion of female labour from branches of industry that are especially unhealthy for the female body or are objectionable morally for the female sex. If that is what was meant, it should have been said so.[1]

While Marx appears to be concerned to remove the ambiguity, his remarks are not appropriate or adequate to a question of such significance to the development of the whole working class movement and in particular to a question over which the movement was already deeply divided. He does not launch into a polemic arguing that socialists should be in favour of the right of women to work as well as demanding an improvement in the working conditions of all workers, but chides the authors for failing to make clear what type of restriction they wanted to be made on female labour. The clarity that Marx was insisting on was semantic rather than political.

This stance was peculiarly indecisive from a writer who was supposed to be in agreement with the argument 'that the first premise for the emancipation of women is the reintroduction of the entire female sex into public industry'.[2] And this weakness in Marx was to have alarming repercussions in the failure of member organisations of the First and later of the Second International to respond to the growing feminist movement.

But it was the two major developments in the marxist tradition after Marx's death that were to have an even greater impact on the fight for the liberation of women — both at the level of practice and the development of theory. These were the revisionist debate and its aftermath and the experience of the degeneration of the Russian revolution.

Eduard Bernstein opened the revisionist debate in the German Social Democratic Party in 1896 and the views he propounded were defeated at its conference of 1899. However, the reverberations of Bernstein's assault on marxism were felt long after his formal defeat. In Germany his major theses were to be resurrected to form the basis of the majority current within Social Democracy after the first world war. But the most lasting effect of Bernstein's revisionism was in putting a question mark over the nature of the marxist method of analysis.

Bernstein considered that the development of phenomena such as cartels and monopolies and the ability of the working class through its organisations to gain a higher standard of living marked a qualitative change in capitalist society. Capitalism was gradually evolving into socialism, which meant that socialists would have no need to resort to the violence of a revolution. But since the cartels and monopolies had evolved independently of the action of socialists Bernstein was left with a problem over the question of individual action. Why should anyone strive after social change? It became a purely ethical question.

Against Bernstein, Kautsky in Germany and Plekhanov in

Russia argued that the collapse of capitalism was inevitable. The contradictions of capitalism were such, they explained, that very soon it would be faced with an economic crisis that it would be unable to resolve. But while Kautsky's and Plekhanov's polemics were intended as a defence of marxism they raise similar problems to those of Bernstein over the question of individual action. If capitalism was doomed by its very nature to inevitable collapse why should the working class engage in revolutionary action? Their theories left the working class in a position similar to that of Nero, of fiddling while Rome burned.

Plekhanov attempted to deal with this problem by accounting for individual action in terms of historical necessity. The individual puts himself or herself forward as a servant to the laws of social change. He wrote:

> the man who appears to be the cause of a given social phenomenon can and must in turn be considered a *consequence* of those social phenomena which have contributed to the formation of his character and the direction of his will. Considered *as a consequence*, social man can no longer be considered a *free* agent; the circumstances which have determined his actions do not depend upon his will. Hence his activity now appears as an activity subordinated to the laws of necessity.[3]

In other words, Plekhanov considered men to be the links in a material, objective and already determined chain.

On the other hand Bernstein approached the problem from the standpoint of morality. The individual should strive for socialism since socialism represented something that 'ought' to be. In reverting to the 'ought' form – the categorical imperative – Bernstein returned to the days of Kantian philosophy. Kant had insisted on the distinction between a fact and a value – between something that *is* and something that *ought* to be. Thus in separating the analysis of society from the motivation for action Bernstein reproduced within socialist thought Kant's dualist framework.

But dualism was not simply the property of Bernstein.

Kautsky also drew a line between 'the moral ideal, the ethical indignation against exploitation and class oppression' and 'the scientific study of the laws of development of the social organism'[4] which he considered characteristic of marxism. Kautsky and the other defendants of marxist 'orthodoxy' had arrived at this conclusion by resting their claim for the scientific status of marxism on its study of economic facts. Plekhanov echoed Kautsky in his stipulation that 'we have strictly to distinguish between the *economic condition* of a given epoch, *which can be determined with the exactness of natural science and the condition of its ideas*'.[5] Thus dualism took the form in their writings of establishing a disjuncture between the economic base of society and the super-structure of its ideas. As economic necessity provoked individual action, so the ideology of a society was a reflection of its economic relations. Both relations were thus explained as simple ones of cause and effect. In practice this was to reduce marxism to materialism, a point which Plekhanov made explicitly in his statement: 'We work with greater success when we accept nature as the *primary* element and consider mental phenomena as necessary consequences of the motion of matter.'[6]

Marx, however, had developed his method of dialectical materialism as a way of going beyond what he considered to be the false philosophical alternatives of materialism or idealism. That is, he had refused either to reduce everything to the movement of matter, as in the former, or to the mere embodiment of men's ideas, as in the latter. But Plekhanov and Kautsky in combating the idealism of Bernstein also effectively destroyed these gains made by Marx. The impact of revisionism, then, was to push socialist thought back to the pre-marxist period. Bernstein's route went back to Kant while that of Kautsky and Plekhanov led to a form of revamped materialism.

The choice before socialists thus appeared to be between the subjective values of Bernstein's ethical socialism or the objective laws of economic determinism in Kautsky and Plekhanov's version of marxism. A few writers, like Victor Adler of the Austrian social democrats, maintained that Kantian ethics were compatible with marxism. But in all these variations a wedge had been driven into socialist thought between an analysis of the base of society and its superstructure; economics and ideology; objective and subjective values.

The development of economic determinism, masquerading as the ideas of Marx, had a profound effect on the marxist tradition, including on its theorisation of women's oppression. According to the method of economic determinism the most important concern of revolutionaries was the economic relations of society since these were the determining ones. Economic relations, in this definition, were narrowly limited to those of the industrial sector. Thus within this schema women's oppression became an issue peripheral to the class struggle. Firstly, since the family was part of the super-structure and not the base of society, the position of women in the family was considered to be an ideological matter. And since ideology was determined by economics, a change in the attitude to women had to wait on a transformation of the base of society. And secondly, since the arena of political struggle was limited to that of industry, revolutionaries were only interested in the position of women at work and not their position in the home. In short, the liberation of women was fated to follow chronologically the victory of the proletarian revolution, as separate as that had been from the bourgeois revolution which preceded it.

Economic determinism and revisionism, however, while establishing the framework of debate within the socialist movement, did not sum it up. In Germany Rosa Luxemburg and Karl Liebknecht put forward a distinct alternative to the paths provided by Bernstein or by Plekhanov and Kautsky, although they were not entirely free of a weakness for the economic determinist's theory of the inevitable collapse of capitalism. Similarly, there were those within the SPD who attempted to extend its theory and practice on the question of women's oppression. Indeed for a time the SPD developed the most healthy line on this question throughout the European socialist movement fed by an active women's movement that had emerged with the increasing numbers of women at work. In this period before the first world war, August Bebel published his book *Women Under Socialism* (1878) while Clara Zetkin wrote pamphlets on the subject of women's oppression and established the newspaper *Die Gleichheit* ('Equality') aimed specifically at women. But although Bebel's book was heralded as a great theoretical advance, in reality it did nothing to improve on the arguments that Engels had already used in *The Origin of the Family, Private Property and the State*. If anything, his ideas on male and female characteristics were even more rigid and ahistorical than Engels's.

> It is not truly a lovely sight [he wrote] to see women, even with child, vying with men in wheeling heavily laden barrows on railway construction sites. . . . The women are stripped of all that is feminine and their femininity is trampled underfoot, just as our men, in many different types of employment, are bereft of anything manly.[7]

Nor did he have much to suggest for alleviating the oppression of women in the family for he was extremely hostile to abortion and regarded contraception as a public calamity. In truth, Bebel's approach to the question of women, a blend of analysis and heavy moralism, had much in common with Bernstein's.

While Clara Zetkin in her consistent commitment to the emancipation of women had a positive influence on the development of the SPD's practical work, she, like Bebel, was unable to improve significantly on the theoretical understanding of women's oppression. She took as her starting point the position of women workers and put up a strong defence of their right to work. But like Bebel she had little concrete to say about women in the family. On the basis of Engels's analysis in *The Origin of the Family, Private Property and the State* she assumed that the advance of industrialisation would lead to the tasks performed by women in the home being taken over by capitalist enterprise, in other words, that the proletarian family would wither away. And accordingly, as with Engels, her analysis lacks any understanding of the basis of sexism within the working class movement. Consequently, the strategy she put forward was a combination of formal democratic demands and a faith in the ultimate success of the socialist revolution to destroy the exploitation of women workers alongside that of the rest of the proletariat. As such, although Clara Zetkin paid more serious attention to the question of women's oppression than did the economic determinists, her actual strategy for change was not significantly different.

The first world war broke up the Second International and produced within German Social Democracy a three way split. The revolutionaries were in the minority and the majority of German Social Democracy gradually moved towards the positions that had formerly been advanced by Bernstein. The fate of Clara Zetkin's ideas within the revolutionary split-off – the KPD – was tied to that of the communist parties internationally, and as such is more relevant to the discussion of the degeneration of the Russian revolution which follows. However, the effect of the split on the SPD's policy on women's oppression was without question a real setback. All the hard work of Clara Zetkin and the other feminists was swiftly undone as the SPD proclaimed that the existence of married women in industry was a sign of economic distress which would disappear once the prosperity of the working class was secured. But the final irony came when Bernstein's ideas were applied to the problem of establishing a new theoretical basis for the party's work among women. In future women were not to demand the same rights as men but to receive the elevated position within the socialist movement of custodians of Bernstein's subjective values. In effect they were to embody Kantian morality. Thus the women's conference of the SPD in 1921 proclaimed:

> Woman is the born guardian and protectress of human life; that is why social work must seem so very appropriate to her. By allocating to women the task of guarding over human life we simultaneously provide a positive answer to the question whether women have a task in politics at all.[8]

The second development in the marxist movement that we mentioned as having a crucial influence on the theorisation of women's oppression was the experience of the degeneration of the Russian revolution. Of course, the early stages of the revolution gave a tremendous boost to the position of women within the socialist movement. But even at that time the theoretical tasks left by Engels were not taken up and resolved within the Bolshevik Party.

That is not to say that the Russian theoreticians saw the question of women as unimportant but that they considered it, in a similar way to Clara Zetkin, primarily as an empirical one of involving half the proletariat in the revolutionary movement. Thus the writings of Lenin and Trotsky concentrated primarily on encouraging women to take part in Party affairs and attacking the backwardness of the workers and particularly the peasants. The dangers of this approach were not apparent in the early stages of the revolution. But once the problems of economic resources and political control were revealed in all their starkness, the gains made by women, lacking any theoretical underpinning, were among the first to be lost.

Even in the period when the Bolshevik Party took its massive steps in improving the conditions of women its theoretical weakness rendered it incapable of dealing with the total revolution that was taking place in people's lives. Engels's shortcomings on the question of sexuality were magnified a thousand times in the massive upheavals that were taking place. And Lenin and Trotsky, who were able to extend revolutionary theory in other areas, failed in this. Lenin's famous conversation with Clara Zetkin in which he criticised the young communists' enthusiasm for discussing sexual matters testifies to this fact. Trotsky, although realising that a qualitative change was required in all the relations between men and women, still maintained as his starting point traditional notions of masculinity and femininity. The boldest revolution, he wrote, 'cannot convert a woman into a man — or rather, cannot divide equally between them the burden of pregnancy, birth, *nursing and the rearing of children.*'[9]

Alexandra Kollontai alone of the leading Bolsheviks attempted to make the theoretical integration of both the question of sexuality and women's oppression within the revolutionary struggle. She at least began to ask the right questions.

> The problems of sex concern the largest section of society – they concern the working class in its daily life. It is therefore hard to understand why this vital and urgent subject is treated with such indifference. . . . How can we explain the hypocritical way in which 'sexual problems' are relegated to the realm of 'private matters' that are not worth the effort and attention of the collective? Why has the fact been ignored that throughout history one of the constant features of social struggle has been the attempt to change the relationships between the sexes, and the type of moral codes that determine these relationships; and the way personal relationships are organised in a certain social group has had a vital influence on the outcome of the struggle between hostile social classes.[10]

Unfortunately, the discussion that Alexandra Kollontai attempted to provoke within the Bolshevik Party was cut short. For the Stalinisation of the Bolshevik Party brought a halt to all debate and dissension over the future path of the revolution.

The effect of Stalinism was to cultivate within the Bolshevik Party the worst aspects of economic determinism. This, as we have seen, established in the analysis of society a disjuncture between the base and the superstructure. Stalinism added to this a new one – between means and ends. This distinction between the means used to obtain an objective, and the objective itself was applied to the problem of the shortage of resources. If the end was socialism, began the reasoning, then the Party itself could decide for the people what was the most efficient way of getting there. Since economic resources were a pre-condition for social change then the Party had to make sure that those resources were made available by all possible means. The formula became first economic change and then social change when political power could be returned to the people. Although the problem of resources was undeniable, the backwardness of Russia had been an important factor in its revolutionary leap; the division between economic and social change was not an inevitable one. Rather that division represented the emergence of a privileged caste within the Party in whose interest it was to retain political power. The argument over resources became part of the process whereby the power to control their own lives was taken out of the hands of the Russian people. This was most obvious in relation to women.

As Sheila Rowbotham commented when discussing the Russian experience, 'the fate of the ideas about the liberation of women and the slow retreat is a sensitive barometer of the revolution itself'.[11] The effects of the removal of political control from the Russian people was felt most acutely by women. The Genotdel, the independent women's movement which Kollontai had helped to set up and which had encouraged the self-activity of women, was abolished. In the years following, during the 1930s, the gains that women had made in the first phases of the revolution were revoked. Abortion was made illegal. The argument used to justify the move was that an increase in the workforce was of prime importance to the Russian economy. The cult of motherhood was revived. In short, the monopolisation of political power by a bureaucracy ended the attempt of women to gain control over their own bodies. A privileged caste would in future make the decisions for women over questions such as their fertility on the basis of Russia's 'economic' need. But while these measures had a logic behind them, it was one that Marx had never used. It was a travesty of marxism to use 'economic' reasons as an argument against basic political freedoms. For in matters of political control there could be no such divorce between means and ends, while still remaining faithful to Marx's principles. For Marx the abolition of a freedom could never be a means to attaining it in a 'higher' form. The conscious self-activity of the Russian people and not the plans of a bureaucratic caste ruling on its behalf could alone be the basis for the continuing revolutionary process.

But the impact of Stalinism was not limited to Russia. The

theoretical and practical advances made in the first stages of the revolution were lost for whole generations. And so economic determinism, which had first made its appearance as marxist orthodoxy in the debate over Bernstein's revisionism but was for a time dislodged by the theoretical work of Lenin and Trotsky, once more became the common interpretation. Stalinism stood as a heavy weight against further theoretical development within the marxist tradition on the question of women. Since the Russian bureaucracy had put women's liberation as a matter for the agenda of the future communist society and not for the present socialist era, the Communist parties throughout the world could largely ignore the problem.

5.

Marxism and psychoanalysis

The wedge that both revisionism and economic determinism had driven into an analysis of society – between base and superstructure; economics and ideology; industry and the family – restored a dualism at the heart of radical thought. While marxism could claim to explain the relations at the base of society, it appeared that there was a vacuum which required filling by a theory which could explain the realm of the individual, the world of ideas. Psychoanalysis seemed the obvious candidate and had the merit of being considered by society at large as a radical and corrupting theory.

Moreover, the growth of fascism in Europe had shaken the economic determinists' theory that the economic collapse of capitalism would be the signal for the unimpeded march to socialism. The attraction of racism during the extremes of economic crisis in Germany hit hard at the belief that there was a simple causal relation between economics and ideology. There was an obvious parallel between marxism and psychoanalysis in Marx's concept of ideology and Freud's concept of the unconscious and it was here that the first attempts at a fusion between the two systems of thought started. Any development in the understanding of ideology would, of course, be invaluable in providing the groundwork for integrating an analysis of the relations between the sexes into socialist theory. But those radical writers who have attempted to fuse together marxism and psychoanalysis have been faced with huge problems. Both were well developed and drastically different systems. To attempt a synthesis was similar to a rider setting off at a gallop balanced on two horses which tended to pull in opposite directions. Nevertheless a number of writers have tackled the course.

The work of Wilhelm Reich represented the first serious attempt and in many ways he was the harbinger of all the hazards that awaited such a project. Herbert Marcuse and Erich Fromm returned to the problem a generation later and from the differing directions of political theory and psychoanalysis. And more recently, Juliet Mitchell has used psychoanalysis specifically to reappraise the marxist analysis of women's oppression.

But while all four writers applied themselves to the problems that had originated from an economic determinist approach to the analysis of society they nonetheless accepted its dualist heritage. All of them in their own way reproduced the separation of ideology from economics. Wilhelm Reich, Erich Fromm and Juliet Mitchell openly adopted it, and even Herbert Marcuse's conclusions were conditioned by it. For example, Wilhelm Reich explained the relation of marxism to psychoanalysis in these terms: 'Marxism overthrows the old values by economic revolution and materialist philosophy; psychoanalysis does the same, or could do the same, in the sphere of the psyche.'[1] The same method is echoed by Juliet Mitchell: 'in analysing contemporary Western society we are (as elsewhere) dealing with two autonomous areas; the economic mode of capitalism and the ideological mode of patriarchy.'[2] She applied marxism to the first and psychoanalysis to the second. In both the original division between ideology and economics was retained. Similarly Erich Fromm in his turn attempted to use the psychoanalytic theory of the sexual instincts to place them alongside economic relations as the base forces in the social process.

But there is an important difference among the four writers which reflects on the seriousness of each attempt to synthesise the ideas of Marx and Freud. We have already made the point that Freudian psychoanalysis constitutes a coherent system of thought. Now it is necessary to introduce to the discussion the additional factor that psychoanalysis is not only a system of thought, but one which also had a certain dynamic. The development of Freud's theories and their continuing coherence depended on his notion of opposing forces acting within the human mind — that is, on his theory of the libido. A measure of the seriousness with which each writer approached Freudian psychoanalysis is the extent to which they treated it as a dynamic system of thought — the extent to which they confronted the problems posed by the libido theory.

Freud developed the notion of libido in the course of his clinical work as an explanation of the relation between his two major areas of concern, the understanding of sexuality and the unconscious. From his observation of parapraxes (slips of the tongue), the revelations of events by patients under hypnosis and also from his study of dreams, Freud concluded that there were elements within each individual's mind that were repressed from consciousness. He considered that in this idea of repression lay the key to understanding the incidence of neuroses. A neurosis, he suggested, was the eruption in the present life of the patient of an instinct which in the past had been unsuccessfully blocked and which up to that point had been hidden in an unconscious area of his or her mind. This idea of repression and eruption in turn led Freud to put forward the notion that there there was a dynamic principle at work, to which he gave the term libido. The libido, Freud explained, represented the force of the sexual instincts.

Once Freud had established the notion of the libido he developed his own version of a theory of the instincts. To begin with, he considered that the child is born with two sets of instincts, the sexual and the self-preservative instincts. In the early phase of the child's life these two sets of instincts are at one with each other. Through suckling the mother's breast the child obtains the necessary nourishment to keep it alive. However, the self-preservative and the sexual instincts soon become opposed, and it is out of the growing antagonism between them that the structuring of the psyche takes place.

The sexual instincts aim for pleasurable gratification, a

process which Freud referred to as the pleasure principle. At first the ego instincts (self-preservative instincts), have the same aim, but under the influence of reality they learn that pleasurable gratification is not always possible. Since the failure to satisfy a sexual urge causes unpleasant irritation the ego instincts discover that it is necessary to renounce immediate satisfaction in order to guarantee satisfaction in the long term. Freud termed this factor the reality principle. Thus we have the separation of the psyche into two major seats, the conscious and the unconscious, each maintained by different instincts and under the sway of a different principle, and each governed by a different agency, the ego and the id.

As Freud's work developed he continually modified his analysis of the structure of the psyche, and at each move made it less rigid and more complex. He emphasised that the conscious and unconscious regions of the mind do not have fixed boundaries. More and more he considered the force of the id, of the sexual, libidinal instincts, as the primary power within the psyche. Indeed he was to drop the division between the ego and the sexual instincts and explain the ego as a development out of the id.

Accordingly, Freud suggested that the ego was the result of past identifications of the id. In order for the ego to gain any control over the id it had to acquiesce to a large extent in its demands. One way it could do this was by presenting itself as a love object to the id. Thus, for example, the child in thumb-sucking was able to detach itself from total dependency on the mother and therefore to develop its sense of being a separate entity. But in carrying this through the ego was only able to change the direction of sexual energy and not to contain it.

In his later writings[3] Freud introduced his final version of the instinct theory, that is of the opposition between Eros and the death instinct. His abandonment of the original division that he made between the self-preservative instincts of the ego and the sexual instincts of the id paved the way for his understanding of Eros. Eros was the force of life, the instinctual aim of the human organism, as well as all other organisms, to preserve living substance and to join it into ever larger units. But acting against Eros was the death instinct, a force aiming to dissolve those units and return them to their original state of dispersion. Freud's postulate of the existence of these two instincts enabled him to account for the previously inexplicable phenomena of sadism and masochism. In both the sexual instinct took the form of a destructive impulse – in the first directed against the other, in the second directed against the self. Freud believed that these phenomena could now be explained by the combination of the death instinct with Eros, which resulted in a fusion of eroticism and destructiveness.

But while Freud's theory of the instincts underwent these changes and sophistications, the underlying concept that remained constant and gave coherence to those developments was that of the libido. The concept of the libido gave meaning to the opposition between the self-preservative and sexual instincts and later between Eros and the death instinct. It was in terms of the libido that he accounted for the structuring of the psyche into the conscious and unconscious, governed by the agencies of the ego and the id. Freud considered that all these were ultimately reducible to the 'economics' of the libido. What then in more detail was his understanding of this force?

Freud's view of the libido was based on the idea that each human being formed a closed system with a static quantity of energy which could be redirected but not increased or diminished. Similarly, Freud believed that the libido was a form of energy that could not be contained; its force had to express itself in some way, whether it was in sexual pleasure, neuroses, or in its other sublimated and repressed forms. This is clear from Freud's discussion of the libido in *The Introductory Lectures on Psychoanalysis*:

> The quantitative factor is no less decisive as regards capacity to resist neurotic illness. It is a matter of *what quota* of unemployed libido a person is able to hold in suspension and of *how large a fraction* of his libido he is able to divert from sexual to sublimated aims. The ultimate aim of mental activity, which may be described

qualitatively as an endeavour to obtain pleasure and avoid unpleasure, emerges, looked at from the economic point of view, as the task of mastering the amounts of excitation (mass of stimuli) operating in the mental apparatus and of keeping down their accumulation which creates unpleasure.[4]

So elementary was libido to human life that Freud considered that the whole development of civilisation, including men's basic capacity for thought, rested on its sublimation and repression. 'If thought-processes in the wider sense are to be included among these displacements [of libido] then the activity of thinking is also supplied from the sublimation of these erotic motive forces.'[5]

The relation of the repression of libido and the growth of civilisation is best expressed through Freud's concept of the super-ego. This was the last category of physical agency that Freud developed after those of the ego and the id and it is crucial in completing his theory of the unconscious. The concept of the super-ego adds the finishing touches to the relation between sexuality, its repression, the structuring of the unconscious and the development of civilisation. For the super-ego is the inheritance within the psyche of the individual's childhood sexual urges. The repression that took place through the Oedipus complex and prepared the child to enter adult civilised life. The strength of the super-ego, which acts as the continual force of individual conscience, is in proportion to the force of the repressed libido. Freud spoke of the super-ego as 'the expression of the most powerful impulses and most important libidinal vicissitudes of the id'.[6] And in turn Freud considered that the strength of each individual's super-ego in society was an index of the development of civilisation.

Drop the Freudian notion of the libido, then, and the relation between the theory of sexuality and the structuring of the psyche into the conscious and unconscious systems dissolves. This was the dilemma that faced the four writers who tried to combine marxism and psychoanalysis. Wilhelm Reich and Herbert Marcuse retained it, with its problems, in their work, while Erich Fromm and Juliet Mitchell abandoned it.

Fromm's approach boiled down to taking a little of what he fancied from both marxism and psychoanalysis. He dropped the marxist theory of revolutionary change but retained the importance of environment in conditioning the form of human life. Then later, in *The Art of Loving*, he dropped the term sexual instincts in favour of the all-embracing one of love. Indeed by this stage Fromm had even dropped the claim to be concerned in an analysis of the individual and society, preferring rather to give a little sermon on the importance of love. Since at best Fromm's work represented an eclectic rather than a synthetic approach to Marx and Freud his writings contain little, from our point of view, of lasting interest.

Juliet Mitchell's attempt to side-step the problems posed by Freud's theory of the libido and the instincts is more sophisticated than Fromm's. In translating the German term *trieb* as drive rather than instinct she hoped to avoid the biological determinism that lurks within psychoanalysis. Unfortunately, despite the fact that Mitchell insisted that a psychoanalytic theory of the instincts was a humanised one and that as such no comparison was intended between men and animals, in doing so she contradicted what Freud actually wrote. For in introducing his most refined version of the instinct theory in *Beyond the Pleasure Principle* (1920) Freud spent considerable time discussing the instinctual life of the simplest living organisms. And it was from this discussion that he put forward the hypothesis of a life and a death instinct to explain the many characteristics that he considered these organisms had in common with human beings. 'The present development of human beings requires, as it seems to me,' he concluded, 'no different explanation for that of animals.'[7]

Indeed it was a feature of Freud's later writings that he minimised the ability of men to 'humanise' their instincts. He considered that the power of the individual's ego, that is, of human consciousness, was feeble compared to the instinctual urges of the id. So, for example, in *Civilization and Its Discontents* we find Freud talking of the ego as a mere 'façade' of the id.

But in down-playing Freud's concept of the libido Mitchell incurred problems in establishing a clear interpretation of the psychoanalytic theory of the unconscious. For, as we have seen, in explaining the force of the sexual instincts, the libido also made sense of the structuring of the psyche. Consequently, when Mitchell uses the term 'the unconscious' in *Psychoanalysis and Feminism* we are never sure what she actually means by it. Is the unconscious an unchanging feature of the individual's mind, or is it a feature of the mind within patriarchal capitalism that will disappear with its abolition? In the last chapter of *Psychoanalysis and Feminism* Mitchell talked about new structures gradually coming to be represented in the unconscious after a revolution in social relations.[8] But does this mean therefore that she considered that the repression of the libidinal force of the sexual instinct was inevitable in all forms of society? For the Freudian theory of the unconscious is meaningless without the notion of a repression and redirection of sexual energy.

This in turn means that Mitchell's claim to explain the hold of ideology within patriarchal society is severely damaged. For at one point she had argued that the concept of the unconscious was the key to understanding ideology: 'the unconscious that Freud analysed,' she wrote, 'could thus be analysed as the domain of the reproduction of culture or ideology.'[9] But if the unconscious remains a constant within both a patriarchal capitalistic society and a non-patriarchal socialist one then in what way is it a useful concept to explain the hold of ideology? And if the unconscious and ideology are mutually dependent concepts, as Mitchell appears to assume, then presumably ideology will also exist in a non-patriarchal society. But if this is the case, what is the basic difference between the two types of society? Mitchell leaves these crucial questions unanswered.

Similarly, it is unclear where Mitchell stands in relation to the Oedipus complex. As we have seen, the original Oedipal situation

marked the beginning of human society for Freud. But with
Mitchell we are never quite sure whether she meant it to represent
the beginning of human society or of civilisation – something quite
different. However, since on balance she equates patriarchy with
human society more frequently than with civilisation, we will have
to assume this meaning.[10] But if this is the case then the same
argument that can be made against Freud applies equally to
Mitchell. That is, Mitchell is also open to the criticism that the
Freudian Oedipus complex assumes without explanation the
original domination of men over women. On top of this, however,
in dismissing a social and historical explanation of that relation
the Oedipus complex rests on a biological one. In other words,
Mitchell's adherence to the Oedipus complex leads her to the
conclusion that the social and cultural distinctions between men
and women are ultimately reducible to biological differences. Set
against her specific aim to explain by means of psychoanalytic
theory the origins and basis of femininity, such a conclusion, and
the criticism of it, have even more serious implications than they
did for Freud. Perhaps, it might be suggested in her defence,
Mitchell had intended to use a weaker version of the Oedipus
complex? Perhaps, for example, she meant that while it was a
universal feature of all societies up to this point, it would become
redundant within a non-patriarchal one? But if this were so, then
she would have had to make the appropriate alteration to Freud's
theory of the unconscious. For, as we have seen, the Oedipus
complex was a central and not an accidental feature of that theory.
But again Mitchell remains silent.

Ironically, it is Mitchell's critique of other feminist interpretations of Freud which reveals the basic error in her approach to
psychoanalysis. She accused such writers of reading Freud as a
prescriptive account of society. That is, she felt they took Freud to
be saying that women *should* behave in a certain way when in fact
he was analysing how they actually *do* behave. While there is an
element of truth in this, Mitchell deduced from it a mistaken
conclusion. For she took from it justification for a far stronger

claim, namely that psychoanalysis was, by that fact, a science. In other words she accepted without further question that Freud's basic concepts were unbiased, that they were not conditioned by the ideology of a specific culture at a specific historical point in time. However, not only the Oedipus complex but also Freud's theory of the unconscious, of the libido and its repression, were affected by his experience of capitalism, as I shall show later. But even without this, the error of Mitchell's attempt to pluck such theories from Freud's particular conceptual framework and to place them unaltered within a revolutionary feminist one, is clear. They mix just about as well as oil and water.

What then are the implications of this for Mitchell's synthesis of marxism and psychoanalysis? In accepting the scientific status of psychoanalysis to be the same as that of marxism, Mitchell assumed that there was no problem in the relation between them. Consequently she made no provision for reconciling the fundamental differences that exist between them on the nature of human society. Thus she, like Fromm before her, failed in her project. Instead of synthesising marxism and psychoanalysis she treated them as two autonomous bodies of thought, each with a separate function in the analysis of society. And in doing so she reproduced, perhaps in a stronger form that it had ever occurred before, the dualism within radical thought.

In contrast to Juliet Mitchell and Erich Fromm, Wilhelm Reich's work maintains a notion of the libido throughout. His starting-point was to apply a class analysis to the Freudian theory of repression and sublimation of sexual energy. Through his therapeutic work with working class patients he had come to the conclusion that their neuroses were directly connected to their appalling living conditions. Sexual repression was the result of poverty and bad housing. From this premise Reich simplified Freud's concept of repression from a process which was necessary in all societies to one which occurred only in specific ones. In *The*

Invasion of Compulsory Sex-Morality he argued that the repression of sexuality did not exist within primitive cultures and only emerged with the development of class interests. One of the cardinal ways in which a ruling class was able to maintain its domination in society was through the suppression of sexuality. In this way Reich was able to tie together the 'Freudian' concept of the unconscious and the 'marxist' concept of ideology. Repressed sexuality, he argued, expressed itself in the hold of bourgeois ideology and moral sentiments over the minds of the working class. While Reich's move to submit Freud's theories to an historical analysis was a step forward, the conclusions that he himself drew from it in many ways were a step backwards. The way that he theorised the connection between historically specific conditions and a healthy sex life involved a regressive revaluation of Freud's distinction between 'normal' and 'perverse' sexuality.

As we saw earlier, Freud made a distinction between 'normal' and 'perverse' sexuality on the basis of whether it corresponded to adult or infantile forms. Sexuality in the childhood stages was 'polymorphously perverse' and adult sexuality was only established after a long and hazardous journey through the different infantile forms. The sexual urges could return to an early or 'perverse' phase of development. This explained the occurrence of homosexuality, which was a regression or fixation of sexuality at an infantile stage of its development. Reich, however, used his own new understanding of the relation between material conditions and sexuality to draw a much more rigid line than Freud's between its 'normal' and 'perverse' forms. 'Perverse' sexuality, he argued, which included masturbation as well as homosexuality, was an expression of the repression by *class society* of 'normal' genital satisfaction.

> The perverse and neurotic modes of gratification against which society should be protected are in themselves only substitutes for genital gratification and arise only if genital gratification is disturbed or made impossible.[11]

Thus, within Reich's system the primacy of genital sexuality acquired an entirely new dimension. Genital sexuality in itself was a liberating force. Its repression or sublimation had the particular effect of strengthening reactionary forces in society rather than being a necessary precondition for social interchange of any kind. Thus at the same time as making Freud's approach to sexuality more rigid he drastically simplified the process of the redirection of libido. But while the ruling class in capitalist society actively repressed the sex lives of the working class, the latter still retained their revolutionary potential. According to Reich, 'anal urges seem to be much more strongly marked in the middle classes than in the working class, whereas, conversely genital urges are more intense in the working class'.[12] Hence the working class was the revolutionary force in both the sexual and the economic 'spheres'. So, at the expense of knocking off a few corners Reich had managed to combine the marxist theory of class struggle with the importance that Freud gave to sexuality.

Reich used his conclusions on the repression of genital sexuality within capitalism to emphasise the importance of the family as the major arena where this process took place. This emphasis on the family is the most positive and lasting influence that Reich has had on the development of a theory of sexual liberation. He looked at the family primarily through his work on character analysis. A person's character, he argued, was an armour formed as a defence against the hard knocks of reality. But in the sense that it limited the individual's ability to experience life, both within and without in its full intensity, it was a negative development. The family, as a product of definite economic conditions and the structure in which the individual was primarily moulded, forged the type of character which would cling to the status quo. For it was the function of the family to suppress all manifestations of genital sexuality in children and adolescents.

But with his theories on character analysis Reich moved further away from the Freudian concept of the unconscious which was the original starting point for the link up with marxism, via an analysis of ideology. The dynamic for the structuring of the psyche into the conscious, pre-conscious and unconscious systems had, according to Freud, come from the force of the opposition between the reality principle and the sexual instincts. But Reich had denied that this opposition was a necessary one. Consequently he was faced with the task of redefining the psychic make-up. He replaced Freud's model of dynamic interconnecting systems with the three tier construction of the human personality. This construction was analogous to a chocolate fruit cake where all the goodness has sunk to the bottom in the process of cooking. The bottom layer was made up with the individual's natural energies, the enjoyment of work and sociality, or what was essentially the same thing to Reich, the spontaneous sexual urges. These were silted up by the perversions of the second layer which were the result of the sex-negating nature of class society. This layer, he maintained, was equivalent to the Freudian unconscious. And finally on the top, the icing covering everything over, was the individual's character, full of artificial sweetness and politeness.

Given Reich's new definition of the psychic make-up the 'unconscious' no longer explained the hold of ideology but was, rather, a result of it. The 'unconscious' was not a necessary element of the psyche but the historical residue from the damming up of genital satisfaction. If men were instead to express their genital sexuality they could sweep away that residue and realise their natural personality. As Reich himself put it: 'The man who attains genital satisfaction is honourable, responsible, brave and controlled, without making much of a fuss about it.'[13] But if the individual was able to accomplish this, then, through the free expression of genital sexuality repeated at the level of society as a whole, the repressive ideology of capitalism could be brought tumbling down like the walls of Jericho.

With this final step, Reich's logic takes an ironic twist. He had begun with the belief that material conditions caused sexual neuroses and that these had to be changed before a cure could be made. It was because of this premise that he turned to marxism.

However, by developing his theory of the revolutionary force of genital sexuality he eventually arrived at the conclusion that there was no need to fight for the political transformation of society.

'It is not necessary to create anything new,' he wrote towards the end of his life,

> we must merely remove the obstacles that limit the natural social functions, no matter in what form these obstacles turn up. . . . In short, work-democracy is a newly discovered bio-sociologic, natural and basic function of society. It is not a political programme.[14]

His theories of 'work-democracy' and 'biophysical orgone therapy' aimed simply at releasing men's positive life force. By this time Wilhelm Reich had left far behind his early intentions to weld together psychoanalysis and marxism, and yet there was an undeniable logic which linked together his original serious premises and his final bizarre conclusions. That logic was the logic of the theory of the libido as a quantitative sexual force.

While he was prepared to modify or abandon all of Freud's other concepts, Wilhelm Reich maintained a terrier-like hold on the libido theory. And by redefining repression and sublimation in historical terms he elevated that theory to a position of pre-eminence. It was a small step from that to his final obsessive concentration on attempting to measure and analyse the material components of the libido.

The ultimate assessment of Reich's work has to be that it contributed little to countering the weaknesses in radical thought. His 'synthesis' of marxism and psychoanalysis had been a string-and-sticky-paper job, which fell apart once his own enthusiasm for the task dwindled. Although he set himself the important task of analysing the links between economic relations, sexuality and ideology his conclusions dissolved the problems rather than resolving them. Genital sexuality would solve everything. Theory became unimportant and therapy all important. In the same way Reich considered it unnecessary to develop an analysis of female sexuality. Since genital heterosexuality was eminently natural, its free expression would resolve any historical problems in the relations between men and women. Indeed in the course of his life Reich became more and more hostile to the conscious analysis of sexuality. Even consciousness of one's own sexuality was bad and finally he concluded that self-consciousness was at the root of all human malaise.

Like Wilhelm Reich, Herbert Marcuse eagerly grasped the nettle of the libido theory. In his book *Eros and Civilization* he considered that it was possible to integrate the major theses of psychoanalysis with a marxist approach precisely because its essence, the libido theory, was revolutionary. What was required was the reworking of the central psychoanalytic concepts to reveal their revolutionary kernel which had been hidden even from Freud himself. Unlike Reich, Marcuse agreed with Freud that the repression of libido was a necessary condition for cultural advance. However, he drew a distinction between basic repression that is 'the "modification" of the instincts necessary for the perpetuation of the human race in civilisation' and surplus repression, 'the restrictions necessitated by social domination'.[15] Similarly he introduced a sophistication into the reality principle, the restrictive force of reality on the sexual desire, by suggesting that in different historical periods it took different forms. Marcuse argued that these distinctions were an historical extrapolation of Freud's basic ideas rather than external additions to them.

Under the strictures of the performance principle, he suggested, the libido was both spatially and temporally reduced. Firstly, the use of the body primarily as an instrument of labour required the repression of libido and limited its release to a particular and short period of the worker's life – during recreation. Secondly, the libido was concentrated in one area of the body – the genitals – leaving the rest of the body free for work.

By making explicit the form of the reality principle in

capitalist society Marcuse believed that he had made possible the theorisation of a non-repressive civilisation that was derivable from Freud's original theory of the instincts. If the working day and the necessary energy required for labour could be reduced to a minimum, then the reason for the restrictions placed upon the libido by the performance principle would be removed. Since the body would no longer be primarily an instrument of labour then as a whole it could become 'resexualised'. This development in turn would allow the decline of genital sexuality in favour of 'poly-morphous sexuality'. Freud had argued against the possibility of such a release of the libido from the reality principle as it was this which kept its anti-social force in check. Marcuse, however, considered that its release need not be disruptive because it would take place in the form of a 'spread rather than an explosion of libido'.[16] The equation of the resexualisation of the body with the diminishing strength of the reality principle balanced, given Freud's concept of a quantitative amount of libido.

So far so good, but Marcuse still had to deal with Freud's concept of the death instinct. Freud had developed this concept in his later writings, as we have seen, to help account amongst other things for the aggressive elements present in interpersonal relations. Since the existence of a death instinct posed a threat to the mere continuation of civilisation, repressive or non-repressive, Marcuse had to be able to theorise a situation where the development of society involved a weakening of its hold. But first let us recapitulate on Freud's understanding of the death instinct.

The death instinct took its meaning from its relation and contrast to the force of the sexual instinct, or Eros as Freud sometimes termed it. While the tendency of Eros was to bind bodies together in ever larger units, that of the death instinct was conser-vative, to return bodies to their original state of dispersion. There-fore in contrast to Eros the death instinct was a destructive force.

Again, Marcuse applied the premise of a static and quantita-tive amount of instinctual energy to an apparently irreconcilable contradiction within Freud's original theory. He argued that if the body was resexualised then the accompanying release of libido, which had previously been turned back on itself through repression, would weaken the force of the death instinct. For destructive energy, he concluded, could only manifest itself in the space made available by the repression of libido.

But while his application of the economics of the libido was consistent, the form of Marcuse's application involved a corruption and simplification of what Freud had actually understood to be the relation between Eros and the death instinct. Although Freud made a conceptual distinction between Eros and the death instinct he believed that the two forces were inextricably bound together in practice. He wrote in *Beyond the Pleasure Principle* when he first put forward this version of the instinct theory, 'if . . . we are not to abandon the hypothesis of death instincts, we must suppose them to be associated from the very first with life instincts'.[17] Indeed Freud pointed to their coexistence to explain why unimpeded sexual relations within a collective tended to fragment it and to break social ties. The maintenance of such ties involved rather the sublimation of the sexual instincts and their re-emergence in the form of love. It was, therefore, the sublimation not the release of libido that held the destructive force of the death instinct in check. And so Marcuse's simple separation of the death instinct and Eros into one force acting against and one acting for the good of society was quite out of keeping with Freud's analysis.

However, Marcuse was not only faced with the problem of remaining consistent with Freud's basic concepts. If he was actually to synthesise psychoanalysis with marxism he had to do more than theorise the possibility of a non-repressive society. If his theory was to withstand the charge of being utopian, and therefore unmarxist, he had to be able to indicate how such a society could be realised in practice. Specifically, he had to be able to explain why the force of reality should cease, at some historical point in time, its repression of the sexual instinct and allow the resexualisation of the body.

Marcuse's response was to point to two developments. The

first was that of technological advance. Here Marcuse argued that the performance principle, the historical form of the reality principle in capitalist society, was based primarily on the need to overcome material scarcity. The strength and efficiency of the performance principle had been illustrated by the extensive improvements in industry and technology that had taken place in the capitalist epoch. But at the same time this advance removed the problem of scarcity and therefore weakened the basis of the performance principle. When this process becomes complete then the dynamic for repression itself would be removed. As Marcuse himself put it,

> the quantum of instinctual energy still to be diverted into necessary labour (in turn completely mechanised and rationalised) would be so small that a large area of repressive constraints and modifications, no longer sustained by external forces, would collapse.[18]

This all has a pleasing logic, but there is one important snag that I will mention here and return to in greater detail later. Marcuse postulated that these radical changes in the form of social relations all took place without a development in the consciousness of the individuals in society. It all would happen as it were behind their backs, or to be more precise, within the unconscious and instinctual realm of their psyches. Indeed, if anything, as the process developed their consciousness coagulated, for we find Marcuse talking about the reduction of the individual in advanced capitalism to an automaton unable to distinguish 'between war and peace, between civilian and military populations, between truth and propaganda'.[19]

The second development that Marcuse pointed to was the decline of the family. The existence of such a development was vital to his analysis that the super-ego and the accompanying sense of guilt, which were central features of the human condition in civilised society, were on the wane. For Freud had seen both as measures of the increasing level of repression in society. Indeed in *Civilization and Its Discontents* he talked about his intention, to represent the sense of guilt as the most important problem in the development of civilisation and to show that the price we pay for our advance in civilisation is a loss of happiness through the heightening of the sense of guilt.[20]

This sense of guilt originated from the killing of the father at the beginning of human history, but had been reintegrated into the super-ego of every generation since then through the Oedipal situation in the family. The family then was vital to conditioning the strength of the super-ego and thereby, the sense of guilt. Thus if Marcuse could point to a decline in family relations he would reasonably be able to deduce from it that the super-ego, the sense of guilt, and the level of sexual repression were also in decline. But was his crucial premise, that the importance of the family was declining, true?

Marcuse analysed development of the state organisation of society, the provision of state education as signs of the cumulative erosion of the family's social function which lead to what he termed the 'technological abolition of the individual'.[21] But was he justified in taking the undeniable changes in the family as indications of its progressive abolition? Rather, its survival after decades of state education and the creation of a range of state services in conjunction with and not replacing it suggest otherwise. Moreover, Marcuse's announcement of the technological abolition of the individual seems off the mark. Instead, the family appears within an automated society more important than ever as a haven of human and individual values. His conclusion that 'the formation of the mature super-ego seems to skip the stage of individualisation; the generic atom becomes directly a social atom . . .'[22] fits in with his theoretical needs but not, unfortunately, with reality.

Marcuse, then, failed both to theorise a non-repressive civilisation and to analyse how it could be brought about in practice. Freudian psychoanalysis could not be revolutionised. But from the point of view of marxism, his theories are even less satisfactory.

Like Reich, Marcuse's theoretical contortions could be traced to the theory of the sexual instincts and the libido. Despite his protestations it was profoundly un-marxist, and could not be squeezed into a revolutionary framework. By making the libido the dynamic of change Marcuse was faced with the problem that any development took place primarily outside the individual's awareness. For the realm of the libido was the realm of the unconscious. But for Marx a qualitative social change was impossible without the development of a revolutionary consciousness within the proletariat. And so from the very beginning the Freudian theory of the libido and the sexual instincts was irreconcilable with the marxist analysis of revolutionary change. In attempting to reconcile the irreconcilable Marcuse found himself in an ironic situation. He had turned to psychoanalysis as a reaction against the reduction of marxism to economic determinism. But in basing himself on a force, the libido, that acted outside of the individual's conscious activity and replaced it as the force for social change, he put forward a form of psychological determinism. In short, Herbert Marcuse had failed to renounce the dualist heritage.

But is it surprising that the attempts to overcome economic determinism through psychoanalysis should be so unsuccessful? Freud and Marx had a radically different outlook on both the nature of interpersonal relations and the relation of the individual to reality. And, moreover, these differences centred on Freud's sexual instinct theory and Marx's emphasis on conscious activity.

Marx's basic approach was an historical one. But Freud considered that while the instincts might manifest themselves differently in specific historical and cultural conditions they themselves were essentially ahistorical. The instincts were ahistorical because they were not determined by their relation to their object. As Freud explained,

> The object of an instinct is that in or through which it can achieve its aim. *It is the most variable thing about an instinct* and it is not originally connected with it, but becomes attached to it only in the consequence of being peculiarly fitted to provide satisfaction.[23]

So while the object might be subject to historical change the sexual instinct was not. The relation was similar to that of an electrical current to a fitting. The fitting might change, it might be a lamp or an iron, but the electricity that powered it remained unaltered.

Marx's analysis of the relation of the individual to objective reality was totally different. Unlike Freud he considered that it was impossible to separate the object of a relation from the relation itself – human beings from their objective reality. Both were subject to historical change as men acted on reality and by changing it, changed themselves. Consequently human beings were always in the process of transforming the very form of their being. All their relations, including their sexual ones, were subject to historical development. But there was one more crucial element in the process. By acting on reality and changing it human beings developed their consciousness. This development of knowledge, which again stood them in a new relation to reality, was what Marx considered as defining the difference between the human species and animals. In the *1844 Manuscripts* he wrote:

> The animal is immediately one with its life activity. It does not distinguish itself from it. It is *its life activity*. Man makes his life activity itself the object of his will and of his consciousness. He has conscious life activity. It is not a determination with which he directly emerges. Conscious life activity distinguishes man immediately from animal life activity.[24]

With Freudian psychoanalysis this distinction between animal and human life was blurred. Men's ability to regulate their sexual instincts was at best an uncertain affair. Ultimately, Freud's theory of the unconscious put severe limits on the ability of the individual to take conscious control over his or her life. But if conscious control was a limited factor in the life of the individual, Freud considered it to be almost non-existent in a group situation. In *Group Psychology and the Analysis of the Ego* (1921) he wrote,

> . . . when individuals come together in a group all their individual inhibitions fall away and all the cruel, brutal and destructive

instincts, which lie dormant in individuals as relics of a primitive epoch, are stirred up to find free gratification.[25]

Thus to accept Freud's theory of the unconscious and the instincts would in effect require abandoning the marxist theory of revolutionary change. For marxism's central premise was that a development in consciousness not simply at an individual level, but at the level of a whole class, the working class, was possible; and the concept of socialism took its meaning from the idea of collective and conscious control. In short, to synthesise marxism and psychoanalysis was an impossible task.

6.

Why Freud was a pessimistic liberal

What is the significance of Freudian psychoanalysis in relation to the weaknesses in radical thought and the theorisation of women's oppression? Simply that it emphasised the sexual dimension in the relations between men and women? There must be more. While the claim of Freud's theory of the sexual instincts to have universal relevance is too strong, it does contain an element of truth of a more limited kind. For Freud's understanding of the sexual instincts as being beyond rational control does come near to the actual experience of sexuality within capitalist society. Here the spontaneous emotions of love appear to defy attempts at intellectual analysis. What then is this more limited element of truth and how does it relate to Marx's theory of human development?

For Marx every historical period was defined by a development in the mode of production, an extension of human control over nature. The epoch of capitalism represents the development of the productive process on a national and even an international scale. But each development in history has not only its positive but also its negative aspects; a price is paid. Capitalism in extending the realm of production turns all goods into commodities, but in doing so it turns human productive activity itself into a commodity. Society is divided into the buyers and sellers of labour power, the exploiters and producers of capital.

Rather than confirming their control over nature, men's labour in producing goods that belong to others confirms the hold of others over them. And yet the individual is unable to explain that dominance. The exchange of labour for a wage appears as an exchange of equivalents. It appears that wealth creates more wealth without any human intervention. The dominance of people appears rather as the dominance of things, of commodities. As Marx explained in a section of *Capital* entitled 'Fetishism of Commodities':

> the relations connecting the labour of one individual with that of the rest appear, not as direct social relations between individuals at work, but as what they really are, material relations between persons and social relations between things.[1]

Within capitalism men's interpersonal relations deny their social existence. The individual only feels himself or herself when detached from others and society becomes something from which to seek protection. Nevertheless we are dependent on our relations to others and their distorted form structures our very consciousness. As Marx summed it up:

> Estrangement is manifested not only in the fact that *my* means of life belong to *someone else*, that my desire is the inaccessible possession of *another*, but also that in the fact that everything is itself something *different* from itself – that my activity is *something else* and that, finally . . . all is under the sway of inhuman power.[2]

It is this condition of human relations in capitalist society where they take on a reified and alienated existence that Freud described so well in his writings. It is in this sense that he is right when he pointed to the structuring of the mind into an unconscious area and of emotions and feelings that the individual is incapable of explaining rationally. And nowhere was this strength of Freud's work clearer than in his essay on *Civilization and Its Discontents*.

In it Freud analysed the main relationships, which from a marxist point of view defined men's being in the world. Instead of confirming the person's existence and control, he or she feels threatened and alienated. Freud painted this gloomy picture:

> We are threatened with suffering from three directions: from our body, which is doomed to decay and dissolution and which cannot

even do without pain and anxiety as warning signals; from the external world, which may rage against us with overwhelming and merciless forces of destruction; and finally from our relations to other men.[3]

Freud looked at the differing solutions that men raise in the face of these problems. Against the suffering from human relationships the individual can keep himself or herself aloof from other people, or withdraw from them by turning to intoxication. Indeed he considered that this latter response in dependency on drinks and drugs was so frequent that 'individuals and peoples alike have given them an established place in the economics of their libido'. Men can safeguard themselves against a vulnerable dependence on others by controlling their instincts. But 'the feeling of happiness derived from the satisfaction of a wild instinctual impulse untamed by the ego is incomparably more intense that that derived from sating an instinct that has been tamed'. Finally one can try to change the external world. However, Freud was extremely sceptical about the result: 'whoever, in desperate defiance sets out upon this path to happiness will as a rule attain nothing. Reality is too strong for them. He becomes a madman. . . .'[4]

In cataloguing the problems and responses to advanced capitalist society then, Freud ruled out the possibility of revolutionary change. Given this, he was left with the traditional liberal framework and its emphasis on the freedom of the individual from social interference. Freud's form of liberalism, however, had a specific relation to its classical predecessor. The theories of Jeremy Bentham and John Stuart Mill were both optimistic and benevolent. At the heart of liberal theory lay the utilitarian principle which assumed that in a rationally organised society, the happiness of the individual would harmonise with that of the majority. Freud's psychoanalysis rested similarly on the principle of the pursuit of pleasure. But Freud's pleasure principle was not, like that of the utilitarians, at one with rationality. Indeed rationality, in the form of the reality principle, acted in opposition to the aims of the pleasure principle. Nor did the pursuit of pleasure result in happiness. The libido could be redirected unsuccessfully and reappear in the form of anti-social neuroses, or in its inter-connection with the death instinct the release of libido could take the form of aggression and sadism. The traditional optimism of liberalism took with Freud an extremely pessimistic turn – a pessimism which implied a criticism of liberalism itself. Freud's darker version of the pleasure principle portrayed a society where communal happiness was bought in the beginning with an act of murder and maintained at the expense of individual neuroses. As Freud himself stated cynically,

> Human life in common is only made possible when a majority comes together which is stronger than any separate individual and which remains united against all separate individuals. The power of the community is then set up as a 'right' in opposition to the power of the individual, which is condemned as 'brute' force. . . . The liberty of the individual is no gift of civilisation. It was greater before there was any civilisation.[5]

The liberal notion of freedom as the individual's freedom from interference, which Freud echoed in his gloomy fashion, was based on the division of society into the political realm of the state and the private realm of the individual. This in turn reflected the division of individuals themselves into the public citizen and the family figure. The political state recognised the rights of the individual man, the right to protection for himself and his property. The private realm was where the individual exercised his freedom. Marx had criticised this liberal notion of freedom and society in both his writings on Hegel's *Philosophy of Right* and *On the Jewish Question*. In the latter he commented ironically,

> The limits within which each person can move without harming others is defined by the law just as the boundary between two fields is defined by the fence. The freedom in question is that of a man treated as an isolated monad and withdrawn into himself.[6]

But what Marx omitted in his critique was the fact that when liberals spoke of man's rights and inalienable liberty, they meant it quite literally. When Marx pointed out that such freedom was based on private property he failed to mention that a man's private property included his wife. So the right to private property meant in practice not just that the poor were exploited and excluded from the exercise of freedom; it also meant the subjugation of women.

The dynamic for the liberal concept of freedom came from the alienation of social relations. With the development of commodity production a split developed between industry and the family. At the same time the accompanying increase in competition turned the world of business and commerce into a rat race. Freedom appeared much more at home in the privacy of the family than in this social world of hostile powers, as is expressed in the cliché 'an Englishman's home is his castle'. If the man's authority was constantly under threat in his social and business life at least it was secure here. The dependency of his wife and children on him and their isolation in the family circle guaranteed that.

There were liberals as we have seen, such as J.S.Mill, who attempted to reconcile liberal theory with the emancipation of women. But their reconciliation at a formal level belies the actual contradiction that exists between them. Women could not in practice wield the same political rights as men and break from the family while leaving the liberal political framework intact. For that framework depended on the division between politics and the family, the public and the private sphere. Once women threw off the restrictions of the family these divisions would begin to dissolve. The sanctity of men's private life would be defiled if women became public figures. For as part of the social world men would meet women as competitors. No longer would men be able to gain assurance and confidence from the knowledge that, however threatened they were by the business world, they remained the central reference point for their wives' lives. Thus the liberal concept of liberty existed in form alone. Its reality was inequality, not only as the freedom of property owners from those who owned nothing, as Marx had pointed out, but also as the restriction and subjugation of women to the family.

This helps to explain both why Freud was such a pessimistic liberal and the wider significance that his theories had to radical thought than simply describing, in a way similar to Marx, the conditions of alienated existence. In focusing on the sexual relations between men and women Freud highlighted the weak spot of liberal theory. While proclaiming freedom for all it was in fact based on the restriction of women to the sphere of the family. And the sexual relationships which Freud analysed were liable to reflect that unequal power relation between men and women. It was not surprising Freud considered that free sexual expression did not lead to happiness. But in drawing attention to the sexual form of human relations he also revealed an aspect of alienation that had been neglected by Marx. In *Civilization and Its Discontents* Freud described the alienation of the individual who is not only ready 'to exploit [the other's] capacity for work without compensation but who is also willing to use him sexually without his consent'.[7] Was there a relation between this neglect and the extent to which marxism itself had not fully broken from liberal thought?

7.

Alienation, reification and the separation of industry from the family

Having introduced the concepts of alienation and reification into the discussion on marxism and psychoanalysis, the terms themselves need explaining in greater detail. In the *Grundrisse* Marx concentrated particularly on analysing these processes and their connection to each other. So it is useful to quote a section from it at some length:

> The social character of activity, and the social form of the product, as well as the share of the individual in production, are here [within capitalism] opposed to individuals as something alien and material; this does not consist in the behaviour of some to others, but in their subordination to relations that exist independently of them and arise from the collision of indifferent individuals with one another. The general exchange of activities and products, which has become a condition of living for each individual and the link between them seems to them to be something alien and independent, like a thing. In exchange value, the social relations of individuals have become transformed into the social connections of material things; personal power has changed into material power.[1]

Thus alienation and reification are based on three related processes. Firstly, in commodity production human labour, the individual's objectification in the world, becomes an alien activity through the expropriation of its product. Secondly, by turning the capacity to labour itself into a commodity, its value, like that of any other commodity, is expressed in monetary terms. Thus social relations within the production process take the form of relations between material things. Thirdly, while a commodity has two values, its exchange value and its use value, capital is primarily concerned with the first. Its interest in a commodity's use is limited to the fact that, without it, it would not sell on the market. And so the exchange of money appears as the rationale and purpose of the whole social system.

From this we can draw out two points. One, that the concepts of alienation and reification are central to the marxist analysis because they describe the form of productive activity within capitalist society and relate that form to the development of human history. And two, they express the process by which communal relations within commodity production become dehumanised. This latter point in turn provides the link between these concepts and the development of a critique of the reduction of marxism to economic determinism. To recapitulate, the economic determinists reduced the scope of human activity to reflecting market movements. Immutable laws of booms and slumps predicted that with or without human intervention capitalism was doomed to collapse. But through the analysis of reification Marx related this type of outlook to the way that each individual experiences the reality of the capitalist process. Social relations take the form of money relations.

Developing Marx's analysis of reification Georg Lukacs took up this theme. He explains in *History and Class Consciousness* how the dehumanisation of the productive process expressed itself within theory as the separation of facts from subjective values. In the same way as communal life appeared as a relation between things, facts appeared external and detached from all human agency. But 'facts', he argued, are 'nothing but the parts, the *aspects* of the total process that have been broken off, artificially isolated and ossified'.[2]

In this way Lukacs provided the key to understanding the persistence of dualism within radical thought. The alternatives of materialism and idealism represented the impact of reification on the method of analysis – either in Plekhanov's definition of the scientific value of marxism in its study of the 'facts' of the capitalist process or in Bernstein's return to the subjective values of Kant. As he explained,

> When confronted by the rigidity of these 'facts' every movement seems like a movement impinging on them, while every tendency to change them appears to be a mere subjective principle (a wish, a value judgement, an ought).[3]

In summary, then, Bernstein's revisionism and economic determinism represented the two complementary theoretical reactions within the marxist tradition to the immediacy of capitalist social relations.

Lukacs went beyond that immediacy and reintegrated the consciousness of human beings within his theoretical analysis. He saw human beings rather than monetary forces as the authors of history. 'In addition to the mere contradiction – the automatic product of capitalism – ,' he wrote, 'a *new* element is required: the consciousness of the proletariat must become deed.'[4] As such his writings represented a positive development within marxism out of economic determinism, a blow against its degeneration. But he was unable to complete that development.

Lukacs considered there was a positive aspect of the reification that takes place within capitalism, that 'only with capitalism does economic class interest emerge in all its starkness as the motor force of history'.[5] He saw that economic starkness as the result of the depersonalisation of socialised production; but in focusing on this he failed to see the other, complementary, side of that process.

In pre-capitalist periods economic and personal and sexual relations had been thoroughly intermingled. The kinship system had provided the rationale for the division of labour within social production. The tasks that men and women performed were allocated on the basis of their place within that system. For example, grandmothers or young girls had their own specific role within industry that was conditioned by the culture and tradition of that particular society. And when men took wives they did so out of economic as well as emotional necessity.

However, with the generalisation of commodity production, the organisation of collective production on the basis of kin was broken down. The labourer made a 'free' contractual relationship with the capitalist in which blood relation played no part. The kinship system existed, although in a weakened form, outside of the socialised production process. The social and sexual relations of kin became separated and then opposed to the economic relations of production.

This then was the other side of capitalism's 'economic starkness' that Georg Lukacs did not analyse. Consequently he failed fully to comprehend the experience of the individual within commodity producing society: '. . . individuality', he wrote, 'was annihilated by the economic conditions to which it was subjected by the reification created by commodity production.'[6] But individuality was not annihilated. Although the subjective existence of the individual was destroyed in industry as the labourer became one more element in the forces of production it remained alive in the family relations outside. This followed from the dual form and historical development of the process of alienation itself. Marx made this point, although he did not draw out its full implications, in the *1844 Manuscripts* when he said,

> The worker therefore only feels himself outside his work, and in his work feels outside himself. He is at home when he is not working, and when he is working he is not at home.[7]

Indeed the importance of the individual's existence within the family increased with the intensification of alienation within the workforce. And once this opposition between the family and work was established the production process continued to reproduce and generalise that divide through all the social relations of society.

Georg Lukacs considered the 'economic starkness' of capitalism a positive development in that it allowed the proletariat to develop its consciousness of the class basis of capitalism. Marx saw things in a similar way when he described in positive terms the destruction of the kinship system of social production:

> Certainly this connection by means of things is to be preferred to a lack of connection, or merely local association which is founded on a relationship consisting of blood ties, or one of supremacy or servitude; and it is just as certain that individuals cannot dominate their own social relationships until they have created them.[8]

But while the relations of social production were made less immediate, in the sense that they were mediated by the exchange of money, and therefore more subject to analysis, the opposite occurred within the relations of the family. Both Lukacs and Marx failed to see that as social production became detached from the family, these latter relations apparently lost their economic meaning. Stripped of this the family became the realm of the personal and the sexual, emotions that were considered subjective and not susceptible to intellectual analysis. The relations between men and women no longer rested, as in pre-capitalist epochs, on the industrial roles that each played within society but on their own spontaneous and personal feelings of love. But, moreover, because the individual's self-confirmation took place within the family and not the work situation, it was in these terms that individuality became defined. Thus the processes of alienation and reification which revealed the class dynamic of capitalism at the same time plunged individual experience into the obscure depths of the emotional and the sexual.

Unfortunately neither Marx nor Lukacs rose to the task of dispelling this obscurity. Neither fully realised the magnitude of the problems involved in overcoming economic determinism and establishing human beings as authors of history. If the proletariat was to become the self-conscious agent of revolutionary change, the hold of this aspect of reification and alienation had also to be challenged.

In capitalist society, then, the question of individual experience takes on a particular form. In pre-capitalist times, the individual was defined according to his or her place within the kinship system, and by the status of that particular system. But within commodity production while the kinship system remained in a certain form, the contractual relationship determined the individual's position in industry. And the primacy of kin was replaced by the cash nexus. However, since the individual's sense of self was systematically destroyed in the work-place, a crucial tension arose. Individuality was not destroyed but found itself in a crisis of definition.

The problem of the individual – of analysing the nature of individual action – was not limited to marxist analysis but reverberated through all areas of social study. One example of this, which we have already mentioned, is the influence of psycho-analysis, and its system of analysing individual action, on twentieth-century thought. There are, however, many more. Whilst it is impossible to make a systematic critique of modern social thought here, I would nevertheless like to look at a couple more examples which add to the argument. Their selection, one from anthropology and one from sociology, is not entirely random, each having a particular feature which merits attention.

The reason behind the selection of the first example, the anthropology of Margaret Mead, lies in her comparison of primitive cultures with advanced capitalist societies. In her studies, Mead explicitly attempted to draw out the lessons of the one for the other. Unfortunately, while her descriptive account of both forms of society was acute, her analysis of the major social dynamics acting within them was fuzzy. In her work on Pacific Island cultures Mead examined the allocation of social tasks on the basis of sex and age, and the culture and traditions that made them a continuous point of reference for each society. Faced with the cultural and social contradictions of America she set herself the task of applying the findings of her anthropological studies to it. However, at the same time her solutions were combined with the tendency within commodity-producing societies to see self-identity in sexual terms. Consequently she proposed elevating 'sex membership', the polarity between masculinity and femininity, into a general criterion of social evaluation:

> every adjustment that minimizes a difference, a vulnerability, in one sex, a differential strength in the other [she wrote] diminishes their possibility of complementing each other, and corresponds — symbolically — to sealing off the constructive receptivity of the female and the vigorous outgoing constructive activity of the male, muting them both in the end to a duller version of human life, in which each is denied the fullness of humanity that each might have had.[9]

To talk about 'sex membership' in these terms was possible in Pacific Island cultures where it was easily ascertained and confirmed by the variety of social tasks that the individual performed. This was illustrated by the fact that male or female homosexuality caused no problem as long as the person concerned acted the social role appropriate to his or her choice of sexual orientation. But in this sense 'sex membership' was based on a set of functions rather than biology. But in capitalist society the rationale for the division of labour on the basis of kin had been broken down. This left Margaret Mead with the reference of biology alone for the assignment of 'sex membership'. As such her solution to the crisis of personal identity was to emphasise the individual's role in reproduction and to base masculinity and femininity on maternity and paternity. In this scheme, however, homosexuals were not only denied 'sex membership', but human membership as well. In summary then, Margaret Mead's work illustrates, in a striking way, not only the tendency within capitalist society to raise the sexual relation between men and women to a position of general social prominence, but also some of its implications.

Talcott Parsons's work shows the same tendency acting within sociology. His major work *The Family, Socialization and*

Interaction Process is significant both in that it attempted to combine some of the findings of psychoanalysis with traditional sociological study and that it has had a considerable impact on the development of sociology. In it Talcott Parsons argued that the symmetry between femininity and masculinity not only forms the personality of each individual from generation to generation but also all the social structures that make up society. He used the terms 'instrumental' and 'expressive' to describe masculinity and femininity, which like Mead he considered were founded on paternal and maternal functions. Society depended on the inter-action between these instrumental and expressive functions. The function of the father was to link the family to society at large. In his occupational role and as the means of financial support, he devoted himself to the long term economic and social goals for the family's external adjustment. The mother, in turn, was the link between the father and the children. Her function was to express the feelings of the family, to interpret for the father the needs and reactions of the children, and to mediate conflicts and to safeguard the internal solidarity of the family. The continuance of this social patterning was ensured by the nature of adult sexuality:

> . . . the mature woman [he wrote] can love, sexually, only a man who takes his full place in the masculine world, above all in its occupational aspects, and who takes responsibility for a family . . . the mature man can only love a woman who is really an adult, a full wife to him and mother to his children.[10]

The problem is, however, that the terms 'instrumental' and 'expressive' together with that of 'sexually mature' assume what they need to explain. Why should masculinity or femininity take this form? And as one writer has commented, Talcott Parsons's definition of an expressive or instrumental function fitted in with the needs of his theoretical schema rather than the actual tasks themselves:

> For, to express warmth, to be constantly person-orientated and conciliatory, it is clearly 'necessary' that the housewife-wife-mother

not be occupied with such highly instrumental tasks as cleaning the house, budgeting the housekeeping money, laundering the clothes, and throwing out the rubbish.[11]

In a way that is reminiscent of Margaret Mead's anthropology, the definitions of masculinity and femininity assume, in Talcott Parsons's sociology, a stability that is in contrast to all other social relations of capitalism. And as for Margaret Mead the sexual relation between men and women acts as an anchorage for the development of Parsons's system of social analysis. In a world of chaos and change gender appears as the one element of continuity to which individuality can be attached.

8.

The existentialist approach

In the course of the discussion, then, three related problems have emerged. Firstly, the impact of alienation and reification within capitalist society and its expression within theory, including marxist theory. Secondly, the theoretical annihilation of individual action that takes place within an economic determinist outlook. And finally, the tendency within commodity-producing society to view the individual in privatised terms at the same time as giving social prominence to the sexual relation between men and women. In what way can these three problems be resolved within the framework of radical thought?

As we have seen, marxism has been able to take us some distance along that path, but it has also revealed its limitations. One theoretical current which has defined its relation to marxism by the questions it asked, can aid in this task. The work of Jean-Paul Sartre and Simone de Beauvoir posed two of the problems directly. In distancing himself from marxism, Sartre gave this reason: 'marxism has absorbed man into the idea while existentialism searches for man everywhere where he is, at work, in the street, in himself.'[1] Earlier, in *Being and Nothingness* he attempted to analyse the form and the importance of the sexual relationships between individuals asking the question: 'Can we admit that this tremendous matter of the sexual life comes as a kind of addition to the human condition?'[2] At the same time Simone de Beauvoir specifically questioned the nature of the relations between men and women in her classic work *The Second Sex*.

Existentialism has always maintained, literally, a problematic relation to marxism. While he originally considered his work as an alternative theory, Sartre, after developing his ideas considerably, announced that they are compatible with a marxist outlook. But despite this the writings of Sartre and de Beauvoir have remained as an interesting appendix to mainstream marxism and have never been full integrated within it. And that situation will continue until their questions have been fully answered.

In *Being and Nothingness*, the work that is most interesting from the point of view of my investigation, Jean-Paul Sartre related the question of sexuality and desire to a mode of subjectivity, a mode of the 'for-itself'. He used the term 'the for-itself' to express a particular and essential movement of the individual's consciousness. In a similar way to Marx,* Jean-Paul Sartre considered that consciousness cannot exist in isolation. It has to be consciousness of something, a perpetual movement out of itself. But consciousness seeks to trap this movement out of itself in order to experience itself as a being in the world. It was this movement of consciousness that Jean-Paul Sartre termed the for-itself. He believed that the crucial way in which the for-itself attempts to find itself is in interpersonal relations. Individuals attempt to experience and confirm their own existence through the recognition by others of their existence.

By locating desire as a mode of the for-itself, then, Sartre related it to the problem of individual self-confirmation. In doing so he highlighted one of the major problems of Freudian psychoanalysis. Freud's definition of the sexual instinct had been ambiguous; it was unclear how far it was a physiological and how far it was a psychological experience. Given this, psychoanalysis was faced with the interesting problem of why the sexual instinct should have more impact in structuring the individual's con-

---

* 'But man is not merely a natural being; he is a *human* natural being. That is to say, he is a being for himself ... and has to confirm and manifest himself as such both in his being and his knowing.' (K. Marx.)[3]

sciousness than for example, hunger. But Sartre, in explaining the dynamic of sexual desire in terms of each individual's need to experience himself or herself in relation to another, drew a firm line between this position and biological determinism. 'Desire is by no means a physiological accident,' he wrote, 'an itching of the flesh which may fortuitously direct us on the Other's flesh.'[4]

This stands in contrast to Freud who had described the need for sexual expression in terms of the mechanical need to release the build up of sexual energy, and who had seen the sexual instinct as quite independent of the object of desire. But what form of the for-itself does desire take? Sartre considered desire as the movement of consciousness towards experiencing itself as a body; that is, as a body alive in its relation with another, not as dead flesh on a butcher's slab. As he explained: 'my caresses cause my flesh to be born for me in so far as it is for the other flesh causing her to be born as flesh.'[5] In other words, it is the inter-relation of the two bodies that enabled this experience to take place. Sartre thought that through desire individuals also experience themselves in a particular relation to the world. The rub of a shirt against the skin, the warmth of the air, the rays of sunshine all become experienced in an especially acute bodily form.

But in that desire is a mode of the for-itself, Sartre argued that it ultimately expressed the failure of each individual to confirm him or herself in interpersonal relations. He described the sexual act as a form of appropriation. In regarding the other as an instrument of pleasure we reduce them to an object. But in so doing we can no longer experience ourselves through their experience, for we have destroyed their subjectivity. In the disappearance of their subjectivity our own loses its hold on the world. As Sartre describes it, 'I insist on taking the Other's body but my very insistence makes my incarnation disappear'.[6]

Unlike Marx, he saw the relations between individuals as a continuous and perpetual failure. Instead of confirming ourselves and developing our knowledge, our meaning in the world continually escapes us. 'There is no dialectic for my relations toward the other,' he wrote, 'but rather a circle — although each attempt is enriched by the failure of the other.'[7]

But what is the basis of this failure? Sartre located it in the fact that interpersonal relations by their very nature take the form of appropriation. We want to entrap the other's subjective experience of ourselves, he argued, because the other makes us exist. But by trying to entrap it we reduce the other to an object. Sartre considered this the continual movement in the relations between individuals — they always exist as a relation between a subject and an object, never two subjects:

> . . . we can never hold a consistent attitude toward the Other unless he is simultaneously revealed to us as subject and object . . . we shall never place ourselves concretely on a plane of equality; that is, on the plane where the recognition of the Other's freedom would involve the Other's recognition of our freedom.[8]

From this failure, he believed, sprang the other forms of relations between individuals, those of sadism and masochism.

He analysed sadism as the attempt to force the other to recognise one's own subjectivity. But in the victim's look the sadist is reduced to an object with his or her subjectivity in flight. Sadism exists in the failure of desire, but its very existence is the basis of its own failure. Similarly with masochism. The masochist attempts to experience himself as an object in the other's subjectivity. But the masochist, in paying the women who whips him, treats her as an instrument and by that fact exists as the subject in a subject-object relation. Again Sartre's analysis of sadism and masochism as the failure of desire, the failure of self-confirmation, makes an interesting comparison with Freud's approach. Freud explained sexual aggression in men and women by the intertwining of two instincts, Eros and the death instinct. The release of sexual energy in its 'normal' form or as sadism depended on the particular mixture of these instincts at a given point in time, a factor outside both the individual's conscious experience and control. Sartre traced sadism and masochism not to the instincts but to the individual's experience of the failure of self-objectification within interpersonal relations.

But is Sartre's analysis of the inevitable failure of inter-personal relations correct? Is it a universal feature of these rela-tions that in establishing our own identity we always reduce the other to an object – or, as Sartre puts it, that personal experience is continuously structured by the attitudes of subjectivity and alterity? The problem is complicated by the fact that the attitudes of subjectivity and alterity (the reduction of the other to an object) are not distributed equally through all individuals in society. It is more frequent that men appropriate women as instruments for sexual pleasure. Woman on the other hand adopts the attitude of a fascinating and seductive object in the hope that the man will choose her in favour of another. It is this aspect of the problem that Simone de Beauvoir made the object of her book, *The Second Sex*.

She argued that in the relationship between the individual and the other, woman is the supreme Other against which man defines himself as subject. In expressing men's otherness women are denied their own individuality.

> A man never begins by presenting himself as an individual of a certain sex; it goes without saying that he is a man. The terms *masculine* and *feminine* are used symmetrically only as a matter of form, as on legal papers. In actuality the relation of the two sexes is not quite like that of two electrical poles, for man represents both the positive and the neutral, as indicated by the common use of *man* to designate human beings in general; whereas woman represents only the negative, defined by limiting criteria without reciprocity.[9]

De Beauvoir's first task was, quite naturally, to explain how woman had become the Other. Unlike Engels she did not believe that female dependency had emerged in a specific historical period.

> Throughout history they have always been subordinated to men [she wrote] and hence their dependency is not the result of a historical event or social change – it was not something that *occurred*.[10]

De Beauvoir thought that woman from the very beginnings of human society had been the Other. Indeed, she argued, human society began with men and not women. Men through their acts, through their support for the group, first constituted their human as opposed to their animal nature, while women through their biology were locked in animal nature. De Beauvoir considered that in giving birth and suckling children, women performed natural functions rather than social activities. Woman therefore, as a part of nature, came to represent the archetypal symbol of Nature as pure alterity to man's subjectivity. From then on each historical period has reproduced this relation of men to women in the form of subjectivity and alterity.

But was de Beauvoir justified in describing the beginnings of human history in these terms?

Similar objections to those made against the Freudian account of this same event apply to her argument, and if anything with more force. Anthropologists have been prepared to debate whether the earliest social forms were matrilineal or patriarchal, whether or not the roles of the two sexes were equally valued. However, there has not been a single faction who has argued that the only tasks that women performed in primitive human cultures was that of child rearing. Some have argued that, for example, the traditional labour of women in berry and nut picking gave them the most social esteem because it provided the most reliable form of sustenance, others that the men's role in hunting had more prestige in that it involved a risk to life. However, none have presented the suggestion that the labour that women performed at this time was not of economic necessity for the community or that it received no social recognition.

Nor is there general evidence that women's child bearing faculties incapacitated them in primitive cultures to the extent that de Beauvoir assumed. In a situation of generalised dependency on nature and a fight for survival, women's closer proximity to nature through her biological functions would have little social meaning. Rather, child rearing acquires a particular social meaning when a society moves from a situation of generalised scarcity to one in which a significant surplus begins to be produced. Women's dependency on men did not spring primarily from biological incapacity but from the power that came from the securing of the right of inheritance. Men had to make women dependent in order to secure rights over their offspring, in order to secure a continuing hold over a surplus. Patriarchy could not have been the first form of human society since it only acquires dynamic and meaning from the growth of a surplus product.

By making women's biology the primary factor in their attitude of alterity in society, Simone de Beauvoir entered into dangerous waters when she came to discuss the question of female sexuality. She considered the young girl who has not yet experienced sexual urges to be equal to boys of her age. She stressed the similarities between them in their ability to make rational choices and to act upon them. But with the onset of mature female sexuality a qualitative change takes place. Instead of stressing the girl's potential for action, de Beauvoir stresses the woman's passivity. De Beauvoir's woman 'always feels passive: she is caressed, penetrated; she undergoes coition, whereas the man exerts himself actively'.[11]

But the equation of female sexuality with passivity condemns women from the very beginning and for always to alterity. And as such Simone de Beauvoir denied that the first premise of existentialism – that men are free in that they choose and define themselves by their own actions – was valid in relation to women. Moreover, she even reproached the woman who was unwilling to identify her sexuality with passivity by calling it a refusal to act responsibly. The lesbian, for example, does not exercise her freedom; her activity is 'not the positive aspect of her choice, it is the negative'.[12] And ultimately de Beauvoir relegated her to the worst category in existentialist philosophy, those who act in 'bad faith'.

> From this the descent is easy to empty bragging and all the play acting that springs from insincerity. . . . Nothing gives a darker

impression of narrow-mindedness and of mutilation than these groups of emancipated women.[13]

Why should Simone de Beauvoir find herself in this contradictory situation in applying existentialism to the relations between men and women? Perhaps the original categories of existentialism, of subjectivity and alterity, that defined the essential nature of interpersonal relations, were based on a historical reality that neither Jean-Paul Sartre or Simone de Beauvoir had analysed? Or to put it another way perhaps their difficulties lay in their failure to resolve all three of the related problems that were posed at the start of this section?

9.

Women and the development of commodity production

In the same way that Simone de Beauvoir was unjustified in explaining women's alterity in the very origins of human society, she simplified too much in identifying female sexuality with passivity. Literature can testify to the fact that it has not always and everywhere been defined in these terms. For example, while Chaucer's *Knight's Tale* placed woman on a pinnacle of passive purity, his *Miller's Tale* and the figure of the Wife of Bath gave witness to a different type of woman – a woman with an active, if not avaricious, sexual appetite. What then is the truth of Simone de Beauvoir's pronouncement of Woman as the Supreme Other?

In pre-capitalist society women from the upper classes stood at a distance from social life and men sang their praise from afar, like the two knights in *The Canterbury Tales*. But women from the lower orders, the peasantry and the merchantry, were like the Wife of Bath, actively engaged in all forms of social interchange. It was only with the onset of capitalist organisation, when the split between the family and social production became generalised through all the classes and social relations of society that the conditions for women's alterity were developed. It is therefore in analysing the transition of feudalism to capitalism from the point of view of changes in the social position of women that the significance of Simone de Beauvoir's ideas should be revealed.

In the space of the seventeenth century in Britain the social value placed upon women changed remarkably. At the beginning of the century men on the whole regarded marriage a boon, by the end, a bane. On the early period one writer has commented, 'men did not regard marriage as necessarily involving the assumption of a serious economic burden, but on the contrary, often considered it to be a step which was likely to strengthen them in life's battles.'[1]

By 1694, however, Mary Astell was writing *A Serious Proposal to the Ladies* which urged the establishment of monasteries or religious retirements to cope with the apparent problem of growing numbers of unmarried women. Whether or not this was actually the case, the frequency of the theme in the literature of the period indicated that it had become a serious matter in the lives of women. Daniel Defoe's Moll Flanders complained that the marriage market 'has become unfavourable to our sex',[2] while Bunyan's Mr Badman represented the outlook 'who would keep a cow of their own who can have a quart of milk for a penny'.[3]

In the seventeenth century the complexities of social stratification underwent rapid transformation and simplification. This transformation can be most easily appreciated by studying the fate of the journeyman and his wife.

The organisation of industry on capitalist principles began to emerge in this period alongside family and domestic-based industry. This latter type of industry had two main forms. The first, where the goods were produced by the family and for the family, existed mainly among the rural population. This type of industry was the successor of the classical feudal relationship between the lord and the serf, and in many cases the family still rented their land from a large landlord and retained a number of social obligations to him. In the second form, the family consisted of father, mother, children and also household servants and apprentices. The most important example of this form was that of the master craftsman's family which developed within the growing urban population, producing goods for exchange. But already coexisting with these forms of industry was the beginnings of a commodity production where industry was controlled by the owners of capital who hired labourers to produce goods in return for a wage. While these three forms of production coexisted in the seventeenth century, and indeed right up to the latter part of the nineteenth, the ascendancy of the capitalist form was already established by the end of the seventeenth. The most important shift in weight took place between the capitalist form of production and the master system, which in turn was measured by the changing position of the journeyman and his wife.

At the height of the master system the wife of every craftsman shared his work. Household tasks were performed by the unmarried girls and servants, thereby enabling married women to play a role in craftwork. So while women were seldom formally apprenticed into a trade they gained a specialised skill through their marriage to a craftsman. If the husband died the wife would usually carry on the business after him. And indeed the widows of master craftsmen were much sought after in marriage as a way into a specialised trade.

However, as industry became more competitive many journeymen never qualified as masters. And as journeymen worked on their master's premises it followed that their wives were no longer associated with their work. Apprenticeship for men became the only entrance into a skilled trade. For women this produced a crisis in employment.

If the journeyman's guild organisation was powerful enough to keep his wage at a high level the woman could join the growing numbers of women who were idle or engaged in unpaid housework. The growth of wealth from the expansion of industry had made it possible for the wives of masters to cease working and to hire more servants, their dependency becoming a symbol of success.

If the journeyman's wages were low the woman was forced into the unskilled, unorganised 'sweated' industries or into the production of thread and yarn to meet the growing demand from the expanding textile trades. The character of spinning made it particularly adaptable to the requirements of the woman who was also engaged in the tasks involved in running a home. But the income from spinning was too low to make her independent of other means of support. Thus the proletarianisation of the journeyman was accompanied by the weakening of the position of women in social production and their reduction, in the majority of cases, to economic dependency. And it was this change in the position of women which lay behind the drop in the value of marriage at the end of the seventeenth century. Thus the production of goods on the basis of the master system was gradually eroded under the pressure of capitalist competition, the unsuccessful masters joining the ranks of the emerging bourgeoisie, while the journeymen and their wives swelled the growing ranks of the proletariat and the dispossessed.

The seventeenth century thus set the stage for the industrial advances of the eighteenth and nineteenth. The competitiveness of capitalist organisation made it the pivotal form of production. While home-based industry remained, it did so as a supplement to it and very often supplied the raw materials for it. It was predominantly in these supplementary areas of production, for example spinning, that women played their part. Those aspects of the trade which were organised on a capitalist basis, for example weaving, became traditionally male employment.

At the end of the eighteenth century and the beginning of the nineteenth, the invention of new machinery paved the way for the massive extension of industrialisation. With this extension there was a development of the scope of capitalist organisation, and at the same time an increase in the demand for all labour, including that of women. But the developments of the seventeenth century ensured that when women entered the factories, they did so from a position of weakness, not strength — something that the employers were able to use to their own advantage. The social crisis that erupted with the introduction of the power looms illustrates this point well.

Weaving, as we noted earlier, was traditionally a man's job. When the employers replaced the old looms with the new power-driven ones many employed female in preference to male labour because they could pay them a lower rate for the job. The result was violent, and as Charlotte Brontë described in *Shirley*, wherever the employers introduced the new machinery it was met with extreme hostility and riot conditions. The introduction of machinery struck fear into the hearts of the working population not only because in making skill redundant it drove down the level of wages, but because everywhere it threatened the tradition-based division of labour between men and women. On the whole men did not accept the presence of women in the factories, and pitted their strength towards keeping them out rather than improving their pay and conditions. Society in general frowned upon the factory girls, and if the working man could not afford to keep his women at home, like the father of Mrs Gaskell's *Mary Barton*, he tried to send her into some other trade. But disapproval was often too mild a term to describe the emotions of the day. The introduction of machinery and the hectic fluctuations in trade made employment extremely unstable. While men fought each other for jobs, these divisions were not quite so bitter or so violent as when men fought women. Because of their historically weak bargaining position and their economic plight, particularly if they were unmarried or widowed, the employers were at times able to use women not only as cheap labour but even as a strike-breaking force. Engels cited an example of this, although he did not draw out its implications, in his book *The Conditions of the Working Class in England*.

> A mill was set on fire in which female knobsticks were employed in spinning in the place of men; a Mrs M'Pherson, mother of one of these girls, was murdered, and both murderers sent to America at the expense of the association.[4]

The association that he referred to was the workers' organisation. And while this form of activity was its most extreme variant, it was generally true of the period that any form of protection that was developed by the working class was of men and for men.

From the 1830s onwards a series of Factory Acts were introduced restricting the employment of female labour. Up to that point the industrialists had opposed any moves in this direction. But as they began to move from labour extensive to labour intensive forms of production they were more willing to see a reduction, although not eradication, of female labour. The trade union movement on the whole gave its support to these Acts, arguing that they would improve women's working conditions. But since the legislation covered only areas of employment where men and women competed for jobs and not, for example, the sweated industries where mainly women worked, it seems that they did so primarily on the basis of protecting traditional male employment.

However, not everyone in the working class movement believed that women should move out of industry. Some women workers valued the economic independence that their employment had afforded them and they put up a surprisingly strong fight to defend their position in the workforce. Amongst these women, particularly from the textile industry in the North of England, there was a growth of unionisation in this period. However, they tended to form new all women unions rather than joining the already established and predominantly male ones. And it was no coincidence that it was from amongst these women that the suffragette movement gained its working class support in its early days.

But however militant these women were, they were fighting against the tide of working class opinion as a whole. Many working women had been demoralised both by their conditions of work and the hostility of their fellow workers. The disintegration of the working class family, as wives and children went out to work and its members moved to different parts of the country in search of work, was seen by the majority as part of the attack of the ruling classes on their way of life. Thus the protection of the family and the securing of women's place within it was regarded as integral to the fight against the employers and the brutalising effect of working conditions. And gradually the ability of the worker to keep his wife at home became a sign of working class strength, of prosperity, of better days to come.

10.

The rise of individualism: the literary evidence

Capitalist commodity production, then, dealt a body blow to the position of women within the social workforce. Middle class women were almost universally excluded from work and the presence of working class women within the workforce was continually under attack. While it was true that in pre-capitalist periods women had been regarded as inferior to men, it was only with the onset of commodity production that the specific conditions were developed in which women assumed, in the terms of Simone de Beauvoir, the role of the Other. Capitalism split society into two worlds – the world of business, industry and social interchange, and the world of the family. But the two were not symmetrical. Men strove to rule in the first, but failing that were the victors in the second. Women were their foil in both. Family life provided the relief where, after the threats and assaults that social life made on a man's confidence, the woman confirmed his human-ity and subjectivity. Away from the constant fight for survival in the competitive arena of social production his position at the centre of the family's world was guaranteed. Femininity, in capitalist society, takes its meaning from this relationship. Men act, women react, femininity is defined as a response to masculinity. The wife's femininity confirms the husband's masculinity. The more feminine the woman, physically delicate, visually attractive, the more sure is the husband's claim to manhood. In short, women are defined primarily in terms of their sexuality.

This helps to explain why with the beginnings of commodity

production, adultery and sexual licentiousness became the most heinous of social crimes. While the woman should be attractive, she should only actually attract one man, her husband. Her adultery was regarded as a threat not only to private property but also to her husband's social standing. In both taking the sexual initiative and giving herself to a competitor, the adulterous woman struck at the heart of her husband's social pride and confidence. And so in bourgeois society for the first time love became based on the idea of monogamy. Courtly love, its predecessor, had taken its meaning from a very different form of relation between the sexes. First of all, it did not have the wide social application that the idea of monogamous love obtained. Courtly love was the exclusive possession of the upper classes. And secondly it was principally a leisure fantasy of the noble lady – already actually married to her feudal lord – and the aspiring unmarried nobleman. The nobleman gained social recognition not through any contact with the lady but through his pursuit of heroic adventures by means of which he proved his love. In contrast, in capitalist society men and women actually proved themselves through the institution of monogamy, because it was through their love that they expressed their very individuality.

This form of individuality, which was reflected in the emphasis on monogamous love, had wide repercussions at all levels of society. The concept of the individual as a separate entity had emerged with the destruction of the system of social obligation, the kinship system, as the basis of production. Until the seventeenth century each person had been considered as but one element in a total picture. This was illustrated by the use of the term 'the body politic' for the state, because each individual had his or her function and each function was necessary to the health of the entire organism. The king as both the head of the 'body politic' and the representative of God on earth invested all the relations within the state with a divine meaning. It was in this context, forming as it did the cement of most social obligations, that marriage was regarded as a holy sacrament.

With the break up of this system of production and obligation the state became conceived of as the aggregate of separate individuals. Coinciding with this development the rise of Protestantism took its great strength from the fact that it offered the individual an immediate relation with God, freed from the necessities of social mediation. The relations within society as a whole were accordingly divested of their religious meaning. The two central relationships of society, that between employer and labourer, and husband and wife, became institutionalised as a secular 'contract'.

But given its importance to individuality against the secularisation of other social relations, the marriage relationship gathered a peculiar sanctity, although that sanctity was not primarily of a religious character. The attitudes of masculinity and femininity on which it was based became a matter of inviolable importance. The differing social behaviour of men and women was enmeshed in a rigid pattern of custom and etiquette, of what women should do 'if they were ladies' and men, 'if they were gentlemen'. The difference between the two roles were emphasised in almost every aspect of speech and manners. For example, Dr Johnson, the ubiquitous commentator of the eighteenth century, gave this recommendation 'that the delicacy of the [female] sex should always be inviolably preserved in eating, in exercise, in dress, in everything'.[1]

A significant measure of the importance of these developments – the change in the position of women; the rise of individualism; and the growing importance of the relations between the sexes – was the emergence in this period of an entirely new form of literature, the novel. Whereas previous literary forms had concentrated on the use of symbol and the representation of general human types, the novel asserted the primacy of individual experience. The logic of the novel rested on the plot, a series of actions by particular people in particular circumstances, rather than the forms of convention used by earlier literature. But most importantly, the architects of this new form made its subject matter the emotional relationships between men and women.

Samuel Richardson, father of the British novel, brilliantly illustrates this. The characters in his novels, *Pamela* and *Clarissa Harlowe*, were the fleshly embodiment of the stereotypes of masculinity and femininity that we have described above. While classical literature had paid little attention to the experience of emotion and passion in the relations between the sexes, he revealed it in its most minute details, right down to the particulars of his heroine's attire.

Richardson's heroines were also a testimony to the efficacy of the standards of femininity that had been developed within bourgeois society. As a model of femininity, Pamela was young, very inexperienced, and so delicate in physical and mental constitution that she fainted at any sexual advance. Essentially passive, she was devoid of any feelings toward her admirer until the marriage knot had been tied. As Ian Watt pointed out in his excellent book, *The Rise of the Novel*, 'a conspicuously weak constitution was both an assertion of a delicately nurtured past and a presumptive claim to a similar future'.[2]

Richardson's heroine, Pamela, was so successful in both entrapping a wealthy husband and remaining within the boundaries of female virtue that she provoked a fierce debate amongst her readers. The altercation centred on whether she was a glowing example to her sex or a despicable and underhand manoeuvrer who understood the art of luring a man. However, as Ian Watt pointed out, 'the ambiguity need not spring from conscious duplicity on Pamela's part, since it is implicit in the feminine code by which she acts'.[3] For the attitude of femininity is the presentation of oneself as a fascinating object. As an object, the woman is passive, the only meaning of the woman's presence is the one the man confers on it. Therefore Pamela was pure, the evil intentions lay rather with the licentious squire, Mr B, who found her passivity provoking. Thus the definition of femininity as passivity sets in motion a polarity of values based on each sex – woman is spiritual, man carnal, woman emotional, man calculating, woman a force for good, man a force for evil.

Richardson's second novel *Clarissa Harlowe* took this polarity to its logical conclusions. Lovelace, the male anti-hero to the heroine Clarissa, likens man to a spider and woman to the predestined fly. In other words, the masculine and feminine codes find their fullest expression in sadism and masochism. The rape of Clarissa by Lovelace, around which the whole novel revolves, takes place when she is unconscious from opiates, thus symbolising the ultimate development of the feminine sexual role as one of passive suffering. And Clarissa's death, which she stoically awaits, indicates that female sexuality can exist only within a lawful marriage relationship. Typically, Clarissa does not commit suicide, which is far too robust an action, but merely fades away.

The novel has been termed a 'feminine' form. Richardson's writings as an exploration of the web of privatised relations illuminated by the presence of women, justify the use of that term. But there are two other factors that give the term its meaning and further reveal the social significance of the novel. They are the role of women as both readers and writers.

The enforced leisure of women, at least from the upper and middle classes, made them avid readers of the novel. For many it became their staple diet. Gustave Flaubert's classic *Madame Bovary* is an ironic comment on this, by making its subject matter a woman's fateful consumption of romantic novellas. For the upper middle class women who even had housekeepers to organise their domestic affairs, reading became the most important way of passing the time. This was reflected in the increasing tendency of booksellers and writers to address special appeals to their feminine audience. Ian Watt noted this phenomenon in his analysis of the novel.

> John Dunton founded the first periodical avowedly addressed to women, the *Ladies Mercury*, in 1693; and there were many other similar efforts, such as the *Female Tatler* in 1709 and Eliza Haywood's *Female Spectator* in 1744. Addison, too, had set himself out to please the ladies, and Steele had compiled *The Ladies' Library* in 1714, to give them something more edifying

than the frivolous material to which they were so often alleged to restrict themselves.[4]

The novel was, however, a luxury item and therefore read primarily by leisured women. As such the female stereotype that it embodied had a strict application only to them. Nevertheless, it had a wider currency. Popular novellas had a larger circulation than the novels, and it appears that women within domestic service had some opportunities for reading. Indeed the fact that Richardson's Pamela was herself a domestic servant seems to indicate that he considered them part of his audience. But whether or not women from the lower orders read novels, if, like Pamela, they aspired to be a lady, or even to be truly feminine, they had in mind the stereotype that predominates in Richardson's novels.

The enforced leisure of upper and middle class women also gave the impetus for the emergence of women as writers of novels. Jane Austen's novel *Pride and Prejudice* which described in both wry and romantic language the problems that middle class women had in catching the right husband is a classic in more senses than one. However, Jane Austen's novels stopped at the mildly mocking. The second generation of women novelists, George Eliot and the Brontë sisters, were much more critical of the traditional role of women. In many ways, both in the very act of writing itself and through the characters they portrayed, they were the forerunners of the suffragettes. They shared with the majority of the suffragettes the same class background and the same impatience with the social restrictions that went with it. Charlotte Brontë's Jane Eyre longs for the life and freedom of movement that is only open to men of her class. And while in her novel *Shirley* she portrayed the passive female type in the angelic figure of Caroline, it is the character of Shirley who steps outside of social conventions, that comes alive. Similarly, the pale quietly suffering figure of Isabelle in Emily Brontë's *Wuthering Heights* serves to set off the vigorous headstrong character of Katherine. And George Eliot's characterisation of Gwendolen in *Daniel Deronda* is a direct criticism of the superficiality of the life that awaits the woman who has to make a career out of femininity. Ironically, as a descendant of these women novelists, Virginia Woolf has in this century given a display of the incongruous talent of espousing femininism at the same time as conserving traditional feminine values. In an uncannily similar way to Samuel Richardson's she uses the figure of Mrs Dalloway, in her novel *To the Lighthouse*, to shine a light over the rest of the characters. The difference is that her glow in comparison to Clarissa Harlowe's is much more diffuse, sophisticated and indefinable.

The history of the novel, then, illustrates in a number of important ways the changing position of women in society. In presenting in a way impossible in other literary forms the inward life of the individual it was able both to capture and reinforce the growing importance of the intimate relations between men and women. The novel was to literature what psychoanalysis was to become to the sciences.

11.

Marx's theory of human development re-posed

Having analysed the rupture of social relations that took place in the transition from feudalism to capitalism, in particular between men and women, we are in a position to return to the problems of the existentialism of Jean-Paul Sartre and Simone de Beauvoir.

To recapitulate, Sartre in *Being and Nothingness* had analysed interpersonal relationships as the continual failure of the human condition made inevitable by the impenetrable categories of existence in the form of subjectivity and alterity. In *The Second Sex* de Beauvoir had made those categories less abstract by relating them to the position of man as the social subject against the otherness of women. But by her hypothesis that the relations between men and women had always taken this form she denied that the existentialist concept of freedom could be applied to women. Women could not choose and define themselves by their actions because their sexuality sealed their destiny. Female sexuality condemned them perpetually to act out the role of the Other.

But the failure of interpersonal relations and their disintegration into the attitudes of subjectivity and alterity was based on a specific historical reality and not on the essential conditions of human existence as Sartre and de Beauvoir assumed. The impact of alienation and reification on the social relations of capitalist society and the historical working out of these processes in the division between industry and the family and the growing importance of the intimate relations between men and women is the reality on which the categories of subjectivity and alterity were founded. De Beauvoir found herself in contradiction with the basic premises of existentialism because she made the attitudes of masculinity and femininity in commodity-producing society the essential nature of the relations between men and women rather than a particular form in the history of those relations. And in doing so she stepped outside of the boundaries of existentialism by assigning to human beings a pre-existent content. For while Sartre had defined desire simply as the individual's need for bodily confirmation, de Beauvoir had assumed that desire had a specific content according to whether it was a man or a woman who was doing the desiring.

The stereotypes presented in Samuel Richardson's novels give the key to explaining both how desire takes the form of appropriation and why it disintegrates into sadism and masochism. Clarissa Harlowe as the predestined fly to Lovelace's spider illustrated that the the attitudes of masculinity and femininity within capitalist society represented respectively the tendency towards sadism and masochism. The historical reduction of women to passivity within the social process determined the form of desire as appropriation. It is her economic dependency that provokes the woman to present herself as a fascinating object in order to attract a husband and thereby achieve financial security. The man, in turn, faced with the apparently uncontrollable and inhuman forces of social production, looks to the woman to confirm his humanity. But since this relationship is from its inception unequal neither are able to confirm themselves on the same 'plane of equality' as Sartre termed it. The response that the man receives is not from a free subject in the sense that the woman is dependent on him. For the woman, in her turn, the form of desire only confirms her dependency. Thus male sexuality becomes the active use of the woman as an instrument of pleasure and female sexuality the woman's passive abandonment to it.

The man exists in the social world of business and industry as well as in the family and therefore is able to express himself in these different spheres. For the woman, however, her place is within the home. Men's objectification within industry, through the expropriation of the product of their labour, takes the form of alienation. But the effect of alienation on the lives and consciousness of women takes an even more oppressive form. Men seek relief from their alienation through their relations with women; for women there is no relief. For these intimate relations are the very ones that are the essential structures of her oppression.

Femininity, then, is defined by the intimate relations of the family – the woman's relationship with her husband, and also with her children. Whereas men reproduce themselves through their industry women reproduce themselves almost entirely through these interpersonal relations. Thus, women experience themselves as a response to other people's needs – most importantly, their emotional needs. In pre-capitalist times it was different. Then, the woman's involvement in industry was important both to her relation to her husband and her children. Not only did her labour contribute visibly to the productivity of the family unit but she also had her part to play in the industrial training of the children. With the advance of capitalist production the woman gradually lost both these roles. Her position in the workforce was weakened and increasingly the state, through the development of a more comprehensive educational system, took on the industrial training of the youth of society. Thus the role of women in the family devolved primarily into one of giving emotional support.

Since a woman's activity is invested in people rather than in objects, she often has difficulty in establishing for herself a distinct and separate identity; we frequently hear the comment that 'a woman lives for her husband and children'. To put it in existentialist terms, women's 'being-for-others' tends to be stronger than their 'being-for-themselves'. Since women experience themselves principally in physical/emotional/sexual terms, they usually are more conscious of their physical than their mental presence – how they appear immediately to others. This awareness that women have of themselves has important implications for their sexuality, for, in a way, it enables them to experience their sexual presence both as women and as men. As John Berger explained in *Ways of Seeing*:

> Men look at women. Women watch themselves being looked at. This determines not only most relations between men and women but also the relation of women to themselves. The surveyor of women in herself is male: the surveyed female.[1]

It is this coexistence of the two attitudes within femininity that is at the origin of Freud's belief in bisexuality being a more pronounced feature in women than in men.

This discussion on femininity in turn helps to clarify some points on the nature of ideology. The analysis of women's oppression has been closely tied with that of ideology. Liberalism as well as marxism has traditionally considered the women's question as one of changing people's attitudes. But to begin with, what are the various interpretations of the term ideology?

Firstly, ideology has been described literally as a set of ideas. This is the economic determinist's view which assumes that each individual idea can be traced back on a one-to-one basis to the economic reality that caused it. Secondly, there is the outlook, which again can be found in crude interpretations of marxism, that considers ideology to be a set of mistaken ideas. Since the bourgeoisie control the means of dissemination of ideas in society, they control and manipulate the ideology of the working class. Accordingly, a change in ideology could be obtained simply through the effective dissemination of an alternative set of correct ideas. And thirdly, there is the view, in many ways similar to the previous one, that ideology can be changed simply by rational persuasion. This is the underlying understanding of liberalism, which is to be found, for example, in J.S.Mill's belief that women's oppression could be overcome simply by appealing to people's good sense.

In the first two 'marxist' interpretations of ideology it appears that men and women are the passive absorbers or reflectors of ideas that have their origin elsewhere – in either the economic base of society or the minds of the bourgeoisie. In both cases ideology is considered as somehow separate and detachable from the individual's experience. The liberal view, on the other hand, assumes ideology to be based primarily on rational experience – given a good argument it can be changed. None of these views, however, explain the experience of femininity as we have just described it. For femininity – or for that matter masculinity – is not something that is additional to the individual's experience. To be a woman or a man in capitalist society means that one's whole experience is structured in a specific, and different, way. And so ideology cannot be explained as a wrong set of ideas, or even a set of ideas at all since it exists at a level deeper than conscious thought and in many ways determines it. In other words it does not operate simply at the level of rational awareness, as the liberals assumed.

A more adequate interpretation of ideology would be that it is based on real experience that is only partially understood. The forms of masculinity and femininity in capitalist society come from real needs and experiences – the alienation of the worker within industry and his need for emotional support from his wife. The problem is that these relations appear as the most natural and unchanging relations of society, whereas actually they are historically specific. But this experience in itself is not without foundation, for it in turn arises from the process of reification in capitalist society. To explain, Marx analysed reification as the process by which social relations take on the appearance of relations between things. This occurs within commodity production as the exchange of money becomes the beginning and end of all social relations. But reification affects not only the socialised relations of production. For while money is the prime form of mediation, those of the family, in standing opposed to the world of business and commerce, appear as having no mediation – in other words, as being immediate. And by appearing the most spontaneous of all relations it seems impossible to conceive of any development in the intimate relations between men and women. It is this level of reality which most men and women experience. Thus ideology is not derived from wrong ideas or wrong experiences but from different levels of reality.

It is in this sense that we can talk about there being an unconscious. The process of reification structurally excludes a level of reality from thought. In terms of the analysis of the women's question this means that the full experience of femininity prevents women developing a consciousness of their oppression. In other words, women can be unknowing accomplices in their own oppression.

Before developing this understanding of the unconscious let us recapitulate on the initial attraction that such a theory had for writers like Wilhelm Reich, Erich Fromm, Herbert Marcuse and Juliet Mitchell. These writers turned to psychoanalysis because marxism seemed unable to explain adequately the sphere of the individual and the significance of the sexual relations between men and women. Similarly, existentialism took its distance from marxism over its concern for these questions. But none of these writers was able both to achieve his or her aim and maintain a consistent historical approach. Those who adopted Freud's theory of the unconscious thereby committed themselves to a theory which put severe limitations on man's potential for conscious development, while Sartre and de Beauvoir's existentialism assumed that the failure of relations between men and women in capitalist society would remain the pattern in perpetuity. What is required, therefore, is an approach which both maintains Marx's theory of human development but at the same time reformulates it by integrating within it an analysis of the significance of the changes in interpersonal relations and men's consciousness of them.

We may sketch the outline of such an approach as follows. At the first stage of their development human beings reproduced themselves as social beings. Each individual was dependent on the actions of society as a whole. But the ties between individuals were based on the fact of material scarcity and therefore the sociality of the individual was an immediate rather than a conscious relation. The individual was unable to visualise him or herself as separate from the community in which he or she existed. Similarly at this point the sexual relations between men and women would take a spontaneous form, existing as the pure need for pleasurable bodily satisfaction. It is possible that in society at this stage in its development the process of procreation would not be understood and that there would be no concept of paternity.

However, once society began to produce a significant surplus product a qualitative change took place. The relations between individuals began to lose some of their quality of immediacy. Those who appropriated the surplus were less vulnerable to the vicissitudes of nature and were able to distance themselves from the communal relations of dependency. The conditions for hierarchical developments within society were created, including most importantly those of patriarchy. The appropriation of the surplus through generations enabled a tradition of dominance to develop. And it was this tradition that was at the origin of the development of classes within society. The active patterning of the relations between men and women, then, was the initial dynamic for the growing complexity of society. In turn it formed the background for the development of a specifically human culture, founded on the customs and religious practices which echoed and reinforced this active patterning of social relations. Myth and fable recorded for each subsequent generation the form of these relations and so perpetuated them. With the emergence of patriarchy and class division the sexual act accordingly became more and more intertwined with the economic, social and cultural relations of a community. The tradition of marriage within a class, the development of a division of labour on the basis of sex and kin position within the community, removed the sexual act from one of spontaneous satisfaction into a highly structured social context.

It was only with the beginnings of commodity production that another qualitative shift took place in the relations between men and women. We have analysed already the major features of that development. The alienation of labour at the heart of commodity production set up the divide between industry and the family and, in the latter, the relation of subjectivity and alterity between men and women. The accompanying reification of social relations apparently removed the human content from industry and economics from the family. The family in turn became the reference point for individuality, and personal identity became imbued with the attitudes of masculinity and femininity, these two attitudes having been founded primarily on the sexual relation between husband and wife.

Concomitant with these developments in social relations was a qualitative change in people's mental structures. In pre-capitalist societies the most important social relations were those based on kinship. In commodity production the significance of kin was broken down and along with it the overriding importance of tradition. The emphasis shifted towards agreements between individuals – the wage contract in industry and the marriage contract in the family. It appeared that custom had given way to conscious choice. Rationalism, rather than blind belief, was heralded as the spirit of the age. Accordingly, the method of rationalism informed the developing sciences and even religion. But there was a crucial tension. While rational choice was proclaimed to be the basis of social relations there were certain important aspects of society which appeared to be beyond rational control. For, as we have seen, commodity production brought in its wake the reification of social relations. In industry money appeared to beget more money without human intervention, while the sexual relations between men and women appeared to defy analysis. But why should this produce a tension? In pre-capitalist times there was no such analysis of social relations, but then neither did men attempt rationally to understand their society as a whole. They acknowledged that some things were inexplicable. For them myth and fable rather than analysis represented the reality of social relations to the individual mind. In sweeping away these metaphorical representations capitalist society was left with a vacuum which it found hard to fill with an analytical theory. While the realm of individual action was emphasised through the alienation of labour and the divide between industry and the family, it was simultaneously obscured by the process of reification. Capitalism demanded an explanation of the individual at the same time as hindering its development.

This tension, then, between the demand for rational explanation and the repression through reification of a level of reality from thought, explains the structuring of men's minds within capitalist society − the division between the conscious and the unconscious. Liberalism expresses this tension in the distinction it makes between the individual and the collective. For while liberalism bases itself on the inherent reason of the individual at the same time it fears above all the unrestrained action of the crowd. According to this theory the individual's rationality disappears once he or she becomes one of a collective. But this tension expresses itself most clearly within psychoanalysis.

It was no accident that when such an explanation of individual action emerged it emphasised men's sexual relations while proclaiming them to be beyond rational control. For Freud's thesis that the price of civilisation is an increase in the repression of sexual pleasure and the incidence of neuroses comes near to men's actual experience in capitalist society. But while there is this link between our theory of the unconscious and Freud's there is a most important distinction. Freud's theory claimed universal relevance, ours does not. In our understanding, the structuring of the pysche into a conscious and unconscious area is dependent on the process of reification in capitalist society. If men were to overcome reification then the dynamic for this form of mental structuring would cease.

Reification and its complementary process, alienation, prevent men's self-confirmation in the world. Conversely, their supersession should enable men's self-realisation in the world − in marxist terms the realisation of human freedom. In this sense the marxist concept of freedom stands fully opposed to that of liberalism where the concept actually arises from the experience of alienation in capitalist society and is confined within it. For the liberal, freedom is security from the interference of others and resides within the rational individual. Both these defining features spring from the inability of men to express their sociality in capitalist society, because of their alienation in industry and the failure of the intimate relations of the family.

The liberal concept of freedom dominated political thought, including radicalism, up to the time of Marx; and marxist theory, while representing a qualitative break from the liberal framework, nonetheless retained the vestiges of its umbilical cord. For Marx did not fully analyse the impact of the processes of reification and alienation and therefore adequately prepare the ground theoretically for their supersession. As we have seen, Marx and marxism did not consider the significance of the failure of men's self-confirmation within the intimate relations of the family in capitalist society. The relationship of existentialism to marxism is a reminder of this. For Sartre defined freedom as anguish, the anguish that sprang from the perpetual inability of human beings to confirm themselves in their being and their knowing through interpersonal relations.

What then would the marxist concept of freedom entail if it included the importance of self-realisation within these relations? As we have seen, male sexuality in capitalist society represents the reduction of women to instruments of pleasure and female sexuality to a most intimate form of alienation. Thus if women as well as men are to realise themselves within the world their reproduction within the sexual relation in the form of objects must be overcome. This ultimately entails, then, the destruction of sexuality in the form of appropriation and the polarity of the attitudes of masculinity on which it is based. Polymorphous sexuality, the term that Herbert Marcuse used for sexuality within communist society, but arrived at this time in a conscious and not an instinctual way, therefore represents the next form of the sexual relations of society.

Polymorphous sexuality suggests the possibility of overcoming the supremacy of genital sexuality, the resexualisation of the entire body and in turn the supersession of heterosexual relations as the inevitable social norm. Genital sexuality was based in pre-capitalist epochs on the importance of the social patterning of the relations between men and women to secure, through the production of an heir, the appropriation of a surplus product. While this remains true to a certain extent within the ruling classes in capitalist society, the primary dynamic for genital sexuality lies in the response to alienation, the man's search for relief in the sexual relation with his wife. But with the supersession of the alienation of a commodity-producing society the impetus for genital sexuality together with the social significance of being either male or female will wane.

In this way the positive aspect of the development of individualism in capitalist society becomes apparent. Marxism, even in its better variants, has traditionally seen this process as a totally negative development – that is, in emphasising the individual, social interchange is devalued. But capitalism in separating men's intimate sexual relations from industry also prepared the ground for their conscious control. In other words, capitalism reveals, without itself being able to resolve, people's potential for realising themselves in all aspects of their sociality, in sexuality as well as in productive activity. Individualism within capitalism, then, is a crucial stage in the creation of the individual as a conscious social being, in the development of a balance between human individuality and sociality. For the negation of capitalism in communist society demands that human beings reproduce their sociality consciously rather than in the spontaneous form of the initial stages of human history.

In summary, the patterning of the intimate relations of men and women is a vital element in completing the marxist theory of the development of human consciousness. The changes in their form determine whether human beings experience themselves spontaneously as in primitive society; or whether a level of reality is excluded from conscious thought as in capitalist society; or whether men and women are able to experience themselves consciously through all their relations as in a future communist society. At the same time the extension in the analysis of the processes of alienation and reification to include their impact on human sexual relations completes Marx's concept of freedom by removing from it the last influences of liberalism. For it was unclear how far Marx considered that a revolutionary struggle would require a radical restructuring of *all* the relations of society and how far he assumed that the sexual relation between men and women would remain basically the same. But by basing freedom on the supersession of alienation and reification in all its aspects its realisation becomes dependent on a qualitative change in human sexuality – the replacement of genital heterosexuality by polymorphous sexuality. Freedom in this sense recognises the ability of men and women to take conscious control of their lives. While their actions will still be limited, they will be limited by processes that they have the potential to understand – not by ones whose reality is repressed from thought. Thus the final supersession of alienation and reification enables human beings to become for the first time the conscious authors of the social process.

12.

Marxist economic theory: its application to the contradictions in the position of women in capitalist society

Up to now we have concentrated our approach to marxism on developing its understanding of ideology, on countering the economic determinist tradition of forcing a split between an ideological and an economic analysis. But this is not to say that the basic economic categories that Marx developed in his major works such as the *Grundrisse* or *Capital* are without value. To do so would only be to reinforce the division between economics and ideology that we have argued should be broken down. Rather they are indispensable to developing a detailed analysis of the tendencies operating in relation to the position of women within capitalist society, particularly in its advanced stages. The remaining task, then, is to return to those categories and develop such an analysis in the light of the previous discussion.

Already steps have been taken in this direction, in a series of articles around the theme of 'domestic labour' in capitalism. These articles represent an important attempt to break with one of the effects of economic determinism on marxist economic theory, namely, its limitation of an analysis of 'the mode of production' simply to the relations of industrial production. Against this, they have attempted to break down the assumption that Marx's economic categories were only relevant to the position of the proletariat at the point of production and that the position of women in the home was somehow outside their scope. However, they have been hampered by the fact that Marx himself had not made the relevance of his categories explicit.

The first contribution to this debate was made by Margaret Benston in 1969, entitled 'The Political Economy of Women's Liberation'.[1] In many ways it set the terms of the discussion. In it she attempted to analyse the 'economic roots' of women's oppression in order to show 'that women as a group do indeed have a definite relation to the means of production and that it is different from that of men'. Her conclusion was that women were defined 'as that group of people who are responsible for the production of simple use values in those activities associated with the home and family'.

Following her Mariarosa Dalla Costa in *The Power of Women and the Subversion of the Community*, went one step further and argued that 'domestic work produces not merely use values, but is essential to the production of surplus value ... housework is *productive* in the marxian sense, that is, is producing surplus value'.[2]

Wally Seccombe in 'The Housewife and her Labour under Capitalism' took the opposite point of view and attempted instead to discover the formula for the value of 'domestic labour'. This approach was subsequently contested in two further contributions. The first, 'Women's Domestic Labour' by Jean Gardiner, assessed the factors working for and against the socialisation of housework in capitalism. The second, 'The Housewife and her Labour under Capitalism – A Critique', written jointly by Margaret Coulson, Branka Magas and Hilary Wainwright, disputed the starting-point of the previous writers in the position of women as housewives and argued instead 'that the central feature of women's position under capitalism is not their role simply as domestic workers, but rather the fact that they are *both* domestic and wage labourers'.[3]

This rapid summary of the arguments does nonetheless throw up the main questions that need to be answered. What is the relation of women to the production of labour power? Does the work of women in the home produce value? Is capitalism likely to socialise this work? And what is the significance of the fact that women go out to work as well as working within the home?

Margaret Benston's opening shot in the discussion, that women produce use values, was in fact largely uncontentious. All objects if they have a use have by that fact a use value. And therefore by turning, for example, the eggs, water, butter and flour into a cake housewives do indeed create new use values. But the changing of an object from one thing to another does not necessarily make any difference more or less to the capitalist system, or by that fact render any new importance to the work of women. That contention arose when Dalla Costa suggested that women not only produce use values but also surplus value. Now the production of surplus value is the very raison d'être of commodity producing society, for it is the basis for the accumulation of capital. If it were the case that women produced surplus value then their labour would be of central importance to the capitalist system. And in turn the position of women in the family would be immediately transformed from being a peripheral question, as marxists have traditionally assumed it to be, to one of strategic importance in the overthrow of capitalism. However, using Marx's distinction between productive and unproductive labour, Seccombe countered this suggestion. Nevertheless, he agreed that the work that women perform in the home, for which he coined the phrase 'domestic labour', was necessary and not peripheral to capitalist production. Productive labour, in his reading of Marx, was defined not by the fact of whether or not it was socially necessary labour but by whether it stood in a direct relation with capital through the wage. 'Domestic labour', while socially necessary labour, was privatised and unwaged, and therefore did not produce surplus value. And so he attempted to pursue a new tack to that of either Benston or Dalla Costa, arguing that 'domestic labour' did express a value which was neither surplus value nor merely use value. The point he made was this:

> When the housewife acts directly upon the wage-purchased goods and necessarily alters their form, her labour becomes part of the congealed mass of past labour embodied in the labour power.[4]

Thus, according to this argument the value that domestic labour creates is expressed in the exchange value of the worker's labour power. As such Seccombe believed that he had revealed the formula for establishing the value of 'domestic labour'. The labourer's wage was divided into two parts, A and B:

> Part A to sustain the wage labourer (and his substitutes) while part B sustains the domestic labourer (and her substitutes). . . . Here is the criteria for establishing domestic labour's value: it creates value equivalent to the 'production costs' of its own maintenance — namely part B of the wage.[5]

But as Gardiner argued in her article, there was a fatal flaw in Seccombe's argument. He maintained that his method was a consistent application of the labour theory of value, namely that the wage labourer does not receive back the full value he creates, part of that value being appropriated by the capitalist, but merely the value of his labour power. However,

> he presents the value created by the domestic labourer as actually determined by the value she receives from her husband's wage packet. Thus the mystification of the wage form which Seccombe exposes and rejects in the case of wage labour is then applied unquestioningly to domestic labour.[6]

Furthermore Gardiner drew on the implications of his conclusions:

> If the value housewives create is in fact equal to the value they receive from their husbands' wage packets, capital neither gains nor loses, in terms of surplus value, from domestic labour.[7]

Thus, in the terms of Seccombe's argument, the position of women as 'domestic labourers' represented no particular tension within the capitalist system. Presumably, except for the existence of 'ideological' benefits which arise from the maintenance of the family, capitalism could just as well socialise it as let it remain privatised.

But let's return to the points made earlier about the distinction between productive and unproductive labour and the categorisation of 'domestic labour' as socially necessary.

Seccombe believed that, firstly, because 'domestic labour' was not productive it was not governed by the law of value. And therefore secondly, because it did not have a direct relation to capital there was no particular pressure on it to increase its productivity:

> The domestic labour force, having no direct relation with capital, is only affected by this development peripherally and has not undergone any significant alteration in the organisation of its labour process throughout the entire capitalist epoch.[8]

But is this true? What about the development of the welfare state in twentieth-century Britain? In the creation of state education and the National Health Service the state has taken on tasks, such as the teaching of the young and the care of the sick, which were previously performed by women in the home. Indeed in no advanced capitalist country have these tasks remained domestic ones. What about the encroachment of commodity production into other areas, such as laundering, clothes- and food-making? And what about the period within capitalism, in Britain at the beginning of the nineteenth century, when the rapid advance of industrialisation swept women into the workforce, threatening the very existence of the family, while a haphazard industry of relatives and other working class women mushroomed to take over their domestic work? In his statement Seccombe totally dismissed these phenomena as having no significance.

But does this in fact mean that Seccombe was wrong in classifying 'domestic labour' as unproductive labour and Dalla Costa right after all? In order to resolve that question it is necessary to make a detour. For in the *Grundrisse* Marx talked about a further situation where 'labour may be necessary without being productive',[9] which casts new light on the problem. He was referring to forms of labour which, as in the development of communication, are 'all *general, communal* conditions of production'.[10] In these cases, while not creating surplus value, there was an important relation between the productivity of the labour involved and capital. These conditions of production –

so long as their production cannot yet be accomplished by capital as such and under its conditions – are therefore paid for out of a part of the country's revenue – out of the government's treasury – and the workers do not appear as productive workers, even though they increase the productive force of capital.[11]

But before considering whether the work of women in the home can be included in this category, there is one further important point that Marx made about this form of labour:

> The highest development of capital exists when the general conditions of the process of social production are not paid out of *deductions from the social revenue*, the state's taxes – where revenue and not capital appears as the labour fund, and where the worker, although he is a free wage worker like any other, nevertheless stands economically in a different relation – but rather out of *capital as capital*. This shows the degree to which capital has subjugated all conditions of social production to itself, on one side: and, on the other side, hence, the extent to which social reproductive wealth has been *capitalised,* and all needs are satisfied through exchange form . . .[12]

In other words, Marx considered that the tendency of capitalist production was to eradicate such forms of socially necessary labour and to bring them under the hegemony of capital. The interesting point is that Marx and Engels had already described the effect of such a tendency on the position on women in the home. For example, in *The Origin of the Family, Private Property and the State* Engels had referred to

> [the] result of modern large-scale industry, which not only permits of the participation of women in production, but actually calls for it and, moreover, strives to convert private domestic work also into a public industry.[13]

Later Clara Zetkin had based her stategy for German Social Democracy on the accuracy of such an analysis in relation to women.

Clearly this tendency, 'the highest development of capital' as

Marx termed it, has not been fully realised in modern capitalist society either in relation to the position of women within the home or even more generally. Commodity production has only partially taken over traditional female tasks. And although the nineteenth century was marked by the extensive use of women and children in industry, by the early part of the twentieth there had been a qualitative stabilisation of the family. And rather than there being a decrease in state intervention, modern capitalism, particularly in Britain, has been characterised by a massive growth of state-run and financed services. Does this mean that Marx's analysis of such a tendency was wrong, or that its application in relation to the position of housewives was misplaced, or perhaps that there was another tendency at work which he had not accounted for? In order to sort out which is correct we will have to proceed by way of another slight digression about the nature of labour power.

In *Capital* Volume One, Marx made these points about the relation between the value of labour power and the employment of women workers:

> The value of labour power was determined, not only by the labour time necessary to maintain the individual adult labourer, but also by that necessary to maintain his family. Machinery, by throwing every member of that family on to the labour market, spreads the value of the man's labour over his whole family. It thus depreciates his labour power.[14]

From this passage it is clear that Marx defined labour power as the *man's* capacity to labour. For if he had considered that the category of labour power applied equally to women as to men he would have talked rather in this section of the *price* of labour power falling below its value, not that the value itself had dropped. Incidentally Seccombe made the same assumption when he described labour power as playing 'a mediating role between the housewife and capital'.[15]

But why should both Marx and Seccombe make this assumption? Abstractly defined, labour power is the capacity to labour, which women share equally with men. The point is, however, that labour power is an abstraction in a number of senses. In *Wages, Price and Profit*, Marx explained one of these senses. The actual value of labour power is not only determined by the formula which applies to all commodities, namely by the amount of labour time embodied within it, but also by definite historical and social factors:

> There are some peculiar features which distinguish the value of labouring power, or the value of labour, from the value of all other commodities. The value of labouring power is formed by two elements – the one merely physical, the other historical or social. Its ultimate limit is determined by the physical element, that is to say, to maintain and reproduce itself, to perpetuate its physical existence, the working class must receive the necessaries absolutely indispensable for living and multiplying. . . . Besides this mere physical element, the value of labour is in every country determined by a traditional standard of life.[16]

In Britain, the first half of the nineteenth century represented a period when the value of labour power was pushed practically to its physical limits. The introduction of machinery and the instability of the labour market decisively weakened the ability of the working class to keep up the value of labour power against the force of capital to drive it down. But by the latter part of the nineteenth and the beginnings of the twentieth century the working class had considerably developed its organisational strength. And with that strength it developed a tradition of values and expectations. Amongst them, and in pride of place, was the belief that the wage should be sufficient to maintain the worker's wife at home. Henry Broadhurst, secretary of the Trade Union Congress Parliamentary Committee, expressed the feelings of the majority of working men in Britain when he said at the Congress of 1877,

> They [the men] had the future of their country and their children to consider, and it was their duty as men and husbands to use their utmost efforts to bring about a condition of things, where their

> wives would be in their proper sphere at home, instead of being dragged into competition for livelihood against the great and the strong men of the world.[17]

In other words the growth in strength of the working class movement was pitted towards defining labour power as a male capacity and demanding accordingly that their wage should reflect that fact. Thus by the beginning of the twentieth century there had been a substantial increase in the value of labour power, a possible development which Marx had again anticipated in *Wages, Price and Profit*.

> By comparing the standard wages or values of labour in different countries, and by comparing them in different historical epochs of the same country, you will find that the value of labour itself is not fixed but a variable magnitude, even supposing the values of all other commodities remain constant.[18]

But the defining of the position of women in the home was not only reflected in an increase in wages. It was also, and later increasingly so, reflected in an increase of state intervention. Through the development of taxation and particularly through development of devices like the married man's tax allowance and family allowances, the maintenance of women within the home became financed partially through state revenue. Thus the activities of women in the family in fact became part of the 'general, communal conditions of production' that Marx had referred to in the *Grundrisse*. While Seccombe was correct that housewives were not productive workers who created surplus value, nevertheless their work is subject to social pressure, as Marx made clear when talking about this form of labour:

> Incidentally, the state itself and everything connected with it belongs with these deductions from revenue, belongs so to speak to the consumption costs for the individual, *the production costs for society*.[19]

And as part of these production costs women came under pressure to be more productive. To reduce those costs the woman could offset a decrease in the value of labour power by buying commodities at an earlier stage in their manufacture and therefore replacing the necessary labour time embodied in them at a later stage in their manufacture with her own. But the pressure on women to do this was indirect, through a decline in the general living standards of the working class. Housework could have been made much more efficient if it were integrated into commodity production, that is, if it succumbed to the tendency that Marx had analysed as acting on it and other similar forms of labour. But why had this not happened, and moreover why had the maintenance of women in the home actually become part of state finances relatively late on in the development of capitalism?

This brings us to the second sense in which labour power was an abstraction. We have already considered one of its senses, that its value is conditioned by definite historical factors. The second, and more important, sense is that it is an abstraction from the individual's human capacities. The existence of the economic category of labour power defines the labour within society as alienated labour. Alienation entails the dehumanisation of men's life activity, its reduction to wage labour. But it also entails, as we have analysed, the investment of the family and, in particular, the relation between husband and wife with intense personal meaning. In other words, the emergence of labour power as an economic category rests on these twin developments of alienation in the division between industry and the family. Thus Marx's economic theory cannot be detached from the major themes of his social and political writing, and most importantly his concepts of alienation and reification. Indeed Marx attacked such false methods of abstraction in his critique of bourgeois economic theory:

> ... the simplest economic category, say e.g. exchange value, presupposes ... a population producing in specific relations; as well as a certain kind of family.... It can never exist other than as an abstract, one-sided relation within an already given, concrete living whole.[20]

So Marx's understanding of labour power presupposed the analysis of the process of alienation within commodity-producing society. However, as we pointed out earlier, Marx did not fully analyse the second aspect of alienation, the relation of the husband's subjectivity to the wife's alterity in the family.

This brings us to the problem that we posed some time back of the relationship between capitalist enterprise and housework. While Marx had been correct in pointing to the tendency within capitalist society to draw all forms of socially necessary labour into a direct relation with capital he failed to see that there was an even stronger tendency acting against it with regard to housework. In response to the experience of alienation the working class movement resisted fiercely the encroachment of capital into the family. Thus it was the importance that the working class attached to the position of women in the family which helped to hold back, to use Marx's terms, 'the highest development of capital'.

Wage labour and the position of women within the family, then, are the two mutually determining forms that productive activity takes in commodity-producing society. This understanding highlights the dangers of treating Marx's economic categories at a superficial level. To consider labour power and its value primarily in monetary terms can lead to forgetting that it expresses a form of being – ignoring that 'the labouring power of man exists only in his living individuality'.[21] The whole 'domestic labour' debate rather tends in this direction which, of course, is a hangover from economic determinism. The attempt to find the value equivalent of 'domestic labour', which was Seccombe's main preoccupation, reduced the activity of the woman to housework and completely missed the significance of her relation to her husband. Ironically, it was the importance of this relation which prevented the housewife appearing on the market in the first place and her work thereby receiving an exchange equivalent. The fact that the husband's work was waged provided the dynamic for his wife's remaining unwaged.

This failure to see the isolation of women in the home as one side of the same historical process which transformed social labour into alienated labour at the beginnings of commodity-producing society is also reflected in another way in the discussion. That is in the idea that the position of women in the home was a leftover from an earlier form of social organisation. Margaret Benston characterised household labour as 'pre-capitalist in a very real sense',[22] while Coulson, Magas and Wainwright talked about the inability of capitalism to 'carry through the bourgeois revolution in the sphere of the reproduction of labour power' and argued that 'the generalisation of commodity production has turned the domestic unit into an oppressive *backwater*'.[23] The point is, rather, that it was precisely the carrying through of the bourgeois revolution, in the split between the family and socialised production, which resulted in the isolation of women within the home. Gardiner also underestimated the significance of the activities of women in capitalist society and their centrality to its basic processes when she asked whether it was cheaper for capital to socialise housework or to let it remain privatised. Given the nature of alienation there were two factors to consider, not only the concern of the individual capitalist over cost but also, and more importantly, the resistance of the working class which would only allow its socialisation up to certain limits.

In Britain, the limits of the socialisation of the work traditionally performed by woman have been defined historically by two developments, that of commodity production on one side and the creation of the welfare state on the other. Of the two, the development of the welfare state needs to be explained further. The welfare state, with its care for the old and the sick and education for the young, emerged alongside of and articulated with the breakdown of the family into its nuclear components. It both expressed and re-emphasised the importance of the relationship between husband and wife and the social defining of the role of women more closely in terms of the reproduction of labour power.

But the creation of the welfare state and the ability of a section of the working class to maintain their wives at home also represented a particular index of the very development of capitalism itself. These two closely linked phenomena placed institutional limits on the tendency of commodity production to bring all socially necessary labour into a direct relation with capital. In other words the creation of the welfare state added significantly to the force acting against 'the highest development of capital'. In turn the ability of the working class to secure these limitations on capitalist development through its organisational strength encouraged reformism within the working class movement. Indeed it was the initial stages of this process as the working class first tested its organisations at the end of the nineteenth century which gave credence to the revisionist argument that capitalist society could be rationalised until it eventually became socialist. For in a sense, at the level of the wage relation, a rationalisation was taking place.

To explain, the wage relation represents a division on two levels, a division of interests between the capitalist and the worker, and a division of the worker's very existence. The individual capitalist pays the wage in order to gain the use of the worker's labour power. He is not concerned with that part of the worker's existence which the wage goes towards sustaining. But for the worker this part of his life is most important. Thus both the demand for higher wages and better conditions of family life spring directly from the experience of waged labour. However, because of the relation of the individual capitalist's interests to that of the worker it is only the first, the level of the wage, that is decided between them. Accordingly wages have traditionally been negotiated at the level of the factory, or perhaps the industry. But while the individual capitalist is not concerned about the conditions in which the worker reproduces his labour power it becomes a matter of importance from the point of view of capital as a whole. The technological advance of the capitalist mode of production demands a certain type and quality of labour power. Thus while the securing of the position of women in the family and the development of welfare state provisions represent a partial meeting of the demands of the working class they also hold a wider significance. They represent the development of a relation of forces between the working class and the bourgeoisie at a national level – that is not simply at the level of the factory or industry – and its outcome in the division of labour between the housewife and the welfare state in the reproduction of labour power.

In what sense does this represent a rationalisation of the wage relation? Firstly, it means the opening up of this new point of contact between the bourgeoisie and the proletariat at a national level. Secondly it means the development of an interest by the bourgeoisie in the second aspect of the worker's life, the conditions of the reproduction of his labour power, which was previously excluded from the wage relation. This interest is mediated by the welfare state and the position of women in the family. And thirdly, the financing of the welfare state becomes, alongide the maintenance of women in the home, part of 'the production costs of society'.

Although these developments around the emergence of the welfare state were rooted in the spontaneous reaction of the working class to its conditions of existence, they could not come about spontaneously. They were dependent on the organised strength of the trade union movement and, more particularly, the creation of the Labour Party as the centralisation of that strength at a national level. Thus, underlying the origins of the Labour Party was the process whereby the wage relation between the proletariat and the bourgeoisie was rationalised. Commentators, from the revisionist debate onwards, have pointed to the growth of working class parties and welfare state provisions in developed capitalist countries generally as indications that Marx's basic premise of class struggle was no longer relevant to the conditions of advanced capitalism – that the rationalisation of the wage relation was a rationalisation of the capitalist process.

However, the development of social democracy, as expressed in Britain by the formation of the Labour Party, did not abolish the basic antagonism between labour and capital but merely modified its form. Both the welfare state and the Labour Party represented an integration of the demands of the working class within the basic structures of capitalism. Thus the definition of the Labour Party as the centralisation of the organised strength of the trade union movement at a national level is only a partial one. Its other aspect is its directing of that strength within the framework of the capitalist state, that is, primarily through parliament. In short the Labour Party and the welfare state were simultaneously both a gain and a loss for the working class. But finally, in that social democracy was founded on the intervention of the state in the reproduction of labour power, its fate is tied up with those relations which have emerged in capitalist society to deal with traditional female tasks.

But does this mean that the maintenance of women within the home and the creation of the welfare state in modifying the contradictions of capitalism eases them? If this were the case then the criticism of Seccombe's argument, that the structuring of women within the capitalist economy caused it no particular problems, would apply equally here as well. However, as part of the production costs of society, both the welfare state and the activities of women in the home have to be accounted for within the circulation of capital. If capital is directed into social revenue through taxation, one of two things, or a combination of them, can happen. There can be a decline in the rate of profit as part of the surplus value goes into social revenue. Or there can be an increase in the price of the commodity in relation to its value, to release money in this way. In the second case the country's products becomes less competitive on the international market. At the same time an inflationary process is created as the workers demand a higher wage to meet the increase in the value of their labour power which takes place with the rising cost of commodities. In either variation or combination of them the interests of the capitalist and the working class remain opposed, between a drop in the capitalist's rate of profit or in the worker's standard of living, and the outcome depends on the balance of forces that exist between them.

An illustration of this is the frequent contemporary talk

about the importance of reducing the 'social wage', as well as employing wage restraint. The 'social wage' is arrived at by dividing the total public spending by the number of the population. So in fact a cut in the 'social wage' entails reducing social expenditure in order to both safeguard the rate of profit and the competitiveness of British goods at the same time as reducing the level of the worker's wage. In other words it is an attempt to shift the weight of the production costs of society, including the cost of the welfare state and the maintenance of women in the family, more onto the shoulders of the working class.

The position of women in the economy also poses a contradiction for capitalism in another way. This lies in the fact which Coulson, Magas and Wainwright pointed to, that women are both housewives and wage labourers. Up to now we have not referred to this and merely focused on the position of women within the privatised relations of the home. Does this mean that our analysis is unable to incorporate it? Part of the answer again lies in an understanding of the nature of the wage relation.

As we pointed out before, the individual capitalist was not concerned in that relation about the social responsibilities of the worker. Indeed this is a characteristic feature of the relations between employer and labourer in capitalist society which distinguishes them from industrial relations in pre-capitalist times – in contrast to, say, the relation between lord and serf, or master and journeyman which involved social obligations on both sides. The lord or the master craftsman accepted a certain amount of responsibility for the welfare of the serf or journeyman and his family in return for their services. The relation between the capitalist and the worker is not marked by such reciprocity. Thus the capitalist was not opposed to taking on female labour on the grounds of a woman's social responsibilities. Indeed in that her social definition in the reproduction of labour power made her labour cheap on the market, he was even predisposed in favour of employing her. Her worries over family concerns made her an ideal choice for employment in low paid, routine and repetitive jobs. The original resistance to her employment came rather from the working class itself.

The second force acting in favour of the employment of women came from women already within the workforce. While the tendency in the development of commodity production was to weaken the position of women within socialised production they were never totally driven out. Within certain limited areas in the textile industry, in traditional female tasks such as spinning, in domestic service and in some weakly organised sections of industry, women retained a hold. And although they were a relatively weak section of the organised working class movement they played a part in securing and extending the position of women as a whole within the workforce.

The third factor in Britain and other advanced capitalist countries was the occurrence within the space of the first fifty years of the twentieth century of two major wars. Women were extensively employed at both times. And while, particularly after the first, their numbers were rapidly reduced to pre-war levels to offset a crisis in male employment, their claim to a job was considerably strengthened.

Together these factors made possible a general movement of women into employment – in Britain particularly after the second world war. But women did not move freely into all parts of industry, rather they were structured into quite specific areas which were termed 'women's work' and paid accordingly. This was divided into roughly three major categories. Firstly, women followed those tasks which had been traditionally performed in the family and were gradually transferred to the welfare state, such as teaching, nursing and aspects of social work. Secondly, they entered the new and therefore less tradition-bound industries which sprang up as a result of the impact of the 'scientific revolution' on technology. And thirdly they became employed in most industries where there was a specific type of job whose activities were described as repetitive and requiring manual dexterity. Such jobs mushroomed as conveyor belt techniques of work became widespread. This increase in the number of women employed, then, is the reality behind the contradiction that Coulson, Magas and Wainwright emphasised within capitalism, that women were both housewives and wage labourers. However, while they were correct in their emphasis, they failed to draw out the most important implications of this contradiction.

The definition of femininity within capitalist society rested primarily on the relation of the woman to her husband within the family. Consequently, the growing phenomenon of the working woman threw into crisis that entire female stereotype. And since it found its meaning largely in sexual terms this crisis in turn gave challenge to traditional codes of sexual relations. Consequently, in those periods that have been highpoints of social unrest in Britain in the twentieth century, the twenties and the sixties particularly, we have seen these features in high prominence. Both periods were marked by the search for new definitions of femininity. The twenties toyed with the ideas of the Flapper Girls and the Vamp, and the latter became immortalised in the film success of Greta Garbo. At the same time the new dances of that era heralded a departure from the previous formalities of the social relations between men and women. The sixties not only saw the eruption of a new form of popular music but the announcement of the arrival of the 'permissive society' and the birth of a whole social movement, the Women's Liberation Movement, which made its point of reference the questioning of accepted norms of female conduct. But the crisis of the sixties had a new dimension that distinguished it from that of the twenties. The scale of the involvement of the state in the reproduction of labour power since 1945 made the potential reverberations of such a crisis much larger. And the instability of the family became a matter for growing bourgeois alarm.

These then are the most important aspects of the contradiction between women as housewives and wage labourers which Coulson, Magas and Wainwright failed to consider. Ironically, they themselves admitted that their analysis of the 'transformation of all sexual and emotional as well as economical and political relations, still probably needs to be spelled out'.[24] But the fault was by no means theirs alone; it was constantly repeated in varying forms throughout the 'domestic labour' discussion. For example, Gardiner pointed to the 'other possible explanation' preventing the socialisation of housework which 'concerns the ideological role of the family'[25] and which she could not deal with in her article. Seccombe completely failed to mention the problem of female sexuality. In each, the crucial aspects of women's oppression in the emotional and sexual relations of society are designated as separable 'ideological' questions and, if dealt with at all, superimposed upon an analysis of the economy.

But in the final analysis the weaknesses of these writers were but pale shadows of those of the economic determinists. For most importantly they made the innovation of applying Marx's economic categories to the position of women. Their shortcomings lay in their failure fully to penetrate the superficiality that economic determinism had reduced them to. But once labour power is understood as a term expressing the alienation of productive activity, then the mechanistic divide that has plagued marxism, between 'the ideological superstructure' and 'the economic base' begins to disappear. And with it, the centrality of the oppression of women to the relations of capitalism, both in the family and social production, begins to emerge. This method of approach also reveals the error of the complementary tendency within marxism – the idea that capitalism can be analysed as some form of model, detachable from the actual conditions of its existence. Such an idea removes the interplay of human forces from the picture. But the historical working through of the process of alienation shows how it is the confrontation between two living forces, the bourgeoisie and the proletariat, which patterns the relations of capitalist society. Accordingly, neither the family nor ideology can be seen as imposed on a passive working class, but rather as phenomena it plays a part in forging.

13.

Three social movements: the trade unions, the Labour Party and the feminist movement

The previous chapter dealt with the contradiction in advanced capitalist society between the definition of femininity in terms of women's role in the family and the presence of women in the work-force. While this contradiction is a feature in common to all advanced capitalist societies it is nonetheless structured in a particular way in each. The specific form this takes is determined by the historical interplay of social movements, most importantly the development of trade union organisation, the emergence of a working class party and the struggle of women themselves. Most historical accounts of capitalism have little to say about the significance of changes in the structural position of women in society. For example, it is rare to find any attempt to show the interrelation between the feminist movement and the form that trade union organisation has taken. In this chapter I want to show the inadequacies of such an approach by making a study of a concrete case – Britain in the twentieth century. However, before doing this I want to make a cautionary point. My aim in this project is to argue that despite the traditional assumptions of historians the position of women in society is structured in a definite and significant way and to indicate what factors a comprehensive historical account of British capitalism in the twentieth century should include, rather than actually furnishing such an account at this time.

Having outlined the contradictory dynamics that spring from the position of women in commodity-producing society the logical next step is to look in this section in more detail at the actual form they have taken in the development of British capitalism in the twentieth century. Given the points just made, this means focusing on those social movements which have had most influence in structuring the position of women within society. Of these the three most important are the trade union movement, the Labour Party and the feminist movement.

However, although our concern is the twentieth century, we cannot actually start there. For the beginning of the story lies in the last quarter of the nineteenth. In his account of this period Tom Nairn has termed these years 'the fateful meridian' for their importance in stamping the Labour Party with the character of that generation of the working class. But the period was momentous in more than this sense. For the same social processes that left their mark on the Labour Party spawned at the same time the trade unions in their modern recognisable form and the first wave of the feminist movement.

In 'The Fateful Meridian'[1] Nairn outlined three features that characterised the period. Firstly, that British society was reaping the economic benefits of an Empire which at the same time in military terms had cost it surprisingly little. Secondly, Britain's industry was still thriving on the fact that it had been the first to introduce machinery on a massive scale. And thirdly the period followed in the aftermath of working class defeat in both the Owenite and Chartist movements. These three features in combination resulted in a peculiar social phenomenon, the emergence of a stratum within the working class which identified with those classes above it and yet maintained within its class a social weight far greater than its numbers. In other words the development of a 'labour aristocracy'. As Tom Nairn explains,

> This part of the proletariat was the higher stratum of skilled workers who first organised themselves into trade unions . . . which shared to some degree in the imperial 'feast' and in this way separated itself

from the mass of workers. Thus these workers were drawn toward integration with bourgeois society. . . . Its whole tendency was to distinguish itself sharply from the 'unskilled' mass, but not so sharply from the lower middle-class strata above it.[2]

The influence that the labour aristocracy had on its class was, therefore, a conservative one. Nairn outlined the specific content of that conservatism in the following way –

The ideology of bourgeois 'self-help', the dogmas of free trade liberalism enshrined in the Liberal Party, the various brands of respectability offered by the dissenting Christian sects, the temperance movement, the prevailing respect for hierarchy and 'knowing one's place' (especially if it were not quite the lowest) and so on.[3]

But Nairn failed to mention one important aspect of the Labour aristocracy's conservatism – its unshakeable belief that the place of women was in the home. This stratum of the working class, then, was an important factor in the entrenchment of this idea throughout its ranks. Indeed Henry Broadhurst, who made the speech at the 1877 Trade Union Congress that we quoted earlier about how the trade union movement should direct its 'utmost efforts' at securing women within the home, was one of its leading figures.

Without the influence of the labour aristocracy in this respect, the New Unionism, the organisation of the previously unprotected unskilled workers that began in the last decades of the nineteenth century, could have possibly had a different outcome. For with this new rise of the trade union movement those women who remained in industry began to organise. Sheila Rowbotham records that in 1872 the Edinburgh Upholsterers Sewers Society was established and in 1876 that the London Society of Bookbinders, Upholsterers and Shirt and Collar Makers took their place in the TUC. Both were all-women unions. In 1875 the Female Cigar Makers Union and the Seamers and Stitchers Union were formed.[4] And it was the strike of the matchgirls in 1888 as well as that of the dockers in the following year that received massive public attention and acted as a symbol for the New Unionism of the unskilled. But while the strength of the dockers earned them an enduring position of importance within the trade union movement, the glory of the matchgirls, and the other sections of female labour that they represented, was much more short-lived. For a start the dockers and the other male workers in industry, like the miners and the transport workers, held a strategic place in the economy, while on the whole women workers did not. As we have seen, the development of commodity production in Britain left women, when they were employed at all, in subsidiary sections of industry. And so when it came to organising in trade unions women did not have the same bargaining strength as male workers. But it was the ideology of the labour aristocracy on the position of women in society, and its currency amongst the majority of male workers, skilled or unskilled, that was decisive. Thus the ideas of New Unionism took on many features of the old, and the flowering of women within the trade unions was cut off in its first bloom. Many of the women's unions that had appeared in the last quarter of the nineteenth century did not last into the twentieth. For those that did, their voice within the trade union movement was seldom heard.

But this fateful meridian did more than weaken the voice of women within the movement; it also established a tradition of issues on which the trade unions fought. Rather than taking a position on all the major social issues of the day, the British trade union movement limited its attention to those of wages and conditions of work. The founding of the Labour Party at this time which, it was thought, could raise 'political' as opposed to 'industrial' problems on behalf of the working class, was obviously crucial in setting this tradition. But the fact that trade unionists were now able to see their family life as a private preserve gave credibility to the outlook that the movement had no direct concern with the broader social issues that affected their lives outside work. When it came to the problems of women, who were firmly secured within this preserve, this was doubly the case. And yet, ironically, in doing so they made it extremely difficult for those women who did work to act in the interests of the unions and not be used by the employers against them to weaken them. For women workers were prevented from taking an active part in the labour movement unless the trade unions themselves took up the broader social issues, such as childcare or abortion and contraception facilities, which affected them most acutely. But that tradition of the trade union movement remains a hard one to break. A comment on this is the fact that even in 1974, after discrimination against women had become a well discussed issue, Pat Turner, Women's Officer of the General and Municipal Workers Union, and otherwise generally progressive, could say, 'women's rights cover the whole gamut of the social fabric but, when I am talking about women trade unionists, I am thinking about employment'.[5]

In the same way as women trade unionists were a component in the beginning phases of New Unionism they also provided some of the initial dynamic for the suffragette movement. In the early days of the movement, in the 1890s, suffragettes addressed meetings of women textile workers. And Annie Kenny, one of the leading members of the movement, was herself a textile worker. It was significant, too, that the Pankhursts had their roots in the Independent Labour Party. For the ILP had been influenced by the activities of women trade unionists, and, unlike other political organisations, allowed women to play a role in its affairs. But as with the New Unionism, the influence of women trade unionists within the suffragette movement was cut short. Ironically, the support that women trade unionists had received through the suffragette movement from women outside the working class in many ways had served to distance them still further from male trade unionists. And their decline in social importance at the turn of the twentieth century coincided significantly with the removal of the offices of the Women's Social and Political Union (WSPU), the organisation of the suffragettes, from Manchester to London. With this move the say of working class women in the campaign was considerably reduced. As Andrew Rosen commented on this period of the history of the WSPU in London,

> The link between the WSPU's leaders and its working class members had remained rather tenuous; the women from the East End who were called upon to demonstrate had no representation in the WSPU's inner councils – they were simply asked to follow plans that were made without their being consulted.[6]

While the voice of working class women was on the wane, that of the middle class, and even upper class women in the movement was waxing strong. These women had been attracted to the suffragette movement as a reaction against their conditions of enforced leisure, a position they found particularly intolerable if they were unmarried. And as Constance Rover pointed out, this was the situation of a large minority. For while

> The assumption of the time was that every women would be looked after by a father or a husband, and that marriage was her natural destiny . . . demographic factors made nonsense of this idea. The 1857 census showed that 42 per cent of women between 20–40 were spinsters.[7]

Prior to joining the WSPU many of these women had engaged in social reforming and belonged to charitable institutions as a similar response to their social situation. And as they became the dominant force within the suffragettes, the movement began to echo some of the characteristics of these previous activities. The campaign appeared more and more like a moral crusade aimed to finally rid the world of all evil. Emmeline Pankhurst spoke of a 'Holy War for the emancipation of our sex', while Christabel, her daughter, admonished that 'in the fight against evil, the few are stronger than the many, women stronger than men'.[8]

There was little to conteract these tendencies. The Labour Party on the whole treated the activities of the WSPU as a diversion from the main concerns of the day and only took a firm position on the issue of women's suffrage as late as 1912. At the same time the weight of working class women within the WSPU was further decreased when from 1906 onwards women of all political sympathies were encouraged to join, and not only women from the Labour Party which had previously been the case. Similarly, from then on, a policy of attracting wealthy donors was pursued. Andrew Rosen characterised the campaign in 1912 in these terms:

> . . . social reforms for working class women, let alone 'socialism' had long since ceased to be the primary goal of the WSPU. The Union sought to appeal to women of all social classes, and denied the existence of any fundamental antagonisms between class interests, at least where women were concerned. Reforms that could benefit working class women were but part of the multitude of reforms that would somehow be made law once women could vote – or, rather, once one woman in seven could vote, as such would have been the result of extending the existing franchise to women, the measure so doggedly advocated by the WSPU.[9]

So the battle cry of the suffragettes, 'Votes for Women', was rather as one contemporary wryly rephrased it, only 'Votes for Ladies'. And although the suffragette campaign remained militant, and in its use of tactics such as damaging property and arson became increasingly so, politically it drifted towards the right.

One important exception to this was the activities of Sylvia Pankhurst. Through her work in the East London Federation of the Suffragettes (ELFS) with working class women and her differing political outlook to that of her mother and sister, she showed how the suffragette movement could have had a very different dynamic and potential. For example, in 1913 she spoke at a *Daily Herald* meeting at the Albert Hall on the issue of women's suffrage which at the same time protested against the lock-out of Dublin workers and the imprisonment of James Larkin. And the *Daily Herald*, in announcing the ELFS's formation of a 'People's Army' commented that 'every day the industrial rebels and the suffragette rebels march nearer together'.[10]

But these occasions when the feminist movement and rank and file trade unionists drew strength from each other were rare.

While there was a significant upsurge in rank and file activity from 1911 right up to the end of the General Strike women had remarkably little involvement in it. The weakness of the position of women within the trade unions was one reason for this. Another reason, however, was the fact that the militancy of the working class in this period took its political coherence from the ideas of syndicalism. Accordingly, the tendency within the trade union movement to restrict its organisation to industry and industrial issues was strengthened. On both counts it offered little support to the struggles of women.

As such Sylvia Pankhurst was fighting against the force of the flood of both the labour and the suffragette movement. Whilst most of the labour movement turned a deaf ear towards her call for unity in struggle, Christabel and Emmeline Pankhurst, on behalf of the WSPU, disinherited the ELFS.

Finally with the outbreak of the war in 1914 the suffragette movement completed its rightwards evolution. To a packed Opera House, 'decked with the flags of the allies' and whilst 'a women's band played national airs', Christabel announced the 'great need of a vigorous defence against the German Peril'. Accordingly, after waging for almost two decades a campaign against all political parties, she recommended jingoism as the healer of all differences.

> In the English-speaking countries under the British Flag and the Stars and Stripes woman's influence is higher, she has a great political radius, her political rights are far more extended than in any other part of the world. . . . I agree with the Prime Minister that we cannot stand by and see brutality triumph over freedom.[11]

In this last farcical twist in the history of the suffragette movement, Lloyd George, its former number one enemy, handed the WSPU £2,000 from the Ministry of Munitions to finance a parade asserting women's 'right to serve'. Banners were carried with inscriptions such as, 'shells made by a wife may save a soldier's life' and the WSPU's paper *The Suffragette* was retitled *Britannia*.

The war marked the end of the suffragette campaign, and the vote was granted soon after peace was declared. But these final days of the campaign illustrated how much the paths of the suffragette and labour movements had diverged. At the end of the war Emmeline and Christabel joined the Conservative Party while Sylvia, who had pointed to the possibilities of a very different relationship between the two movements, helped to form the British Communist Party. And yet both movements had emerged in the same social processes at the end of the nineteenth century and represented, if their struggles had been fused, a potentially revolutionary force. It was the sad conclusion, however, that although the suffragettes had been a massive social movement, the labour movement as a whole did not gain from their fight and women within it only indirectly.

But this barren relationship between the suffragette and labour movements, which had its origins in that 'fateful meridian' at the end of the nineteenth century, also turned up in another form. For this period was also crucial in the moulding of the Labour Party. And the tension between the outlook of the mainstream of the trade union movement and the dynamic set up by the suffragettes that existed in this period was expressed within the Labour Party itself. This is in keeping with what Tom Nairn has described as the determining factors in the emergence of a working class party, namely that,

> If it expresses anything, it can only be the underlying historical situation of a class, in relationship to the rest of society, including its consciousness (true or false) of that situation.[12]

And the historical situation of the working class at that time encompassed two contradictory, and ultimately mutually exclusive, outlooks on the position of women. Accordingly, the Labour Party was tossed between those who wanted to define the position of women solely in terms of the family and those who wanted to recognise the position of working women, failing to take a clear stand on either.

This is most clearly apparent in a pamphlet entitled *Women and the Labour Party*, published in 1919. On the one side M.Philips asserted that 'the industrial freedom of the last century . . . has depended upon the staunch loyalty of the women at home';[13] and M.Llewelyn Davies argued in favour of National Endowment for mothers and 'the withdrawal of most married women from the wage market'.[14] On the other hand, A.S.Lawrence in an article entitled 'The Woman Wage Earner' stated that: 'The woman wage-earner wants security — security against sweating — security against unemployment.'[15]

In many ways the issue of family allowances, or Family Endowment as it was originally termed, became the focal point for this debate on the position of women. The main force of the Family Endowment movement, Eleanor Rathbone, was not herself in the Labour Party. However, her conception of Family Endowment was entirely in keeping with the basic premises of social democracy:

> [Family Endowment stands] for a principle, viz. that the economic structure of society should include some kind of direct provision for the financial costs of rearing children, instead of leaving it to be met through the ordinary wage-system on the assumption that normal wages either are, or should be and can be made to be, sufficient to cover the cost of child-rearing.[16]

It was also significant that she gave the following specific motivation for her proposals in the year following the General Strike:

> Most people would also agree that the Family as an institution has a special value at the present time as a bulwark against certain explosive and disrupting forces. A man with a wife and family may talk revolution, but he is much less likely to act it than one who has given society no such hostages.[17]

In short Eleanor Rathbone proposed to rationalise and, in so doing, safeguard the wage relation.

Mary Stocks put forward similar ideas within the Labour Party and in 1926 the ILP adopted the concept of family endowment as part of its 'Living Wage Policy'. However, there was opposition within the Labour Party to such ideas. Beatrice Webb, in a minority submission to the 1919 *Report of the War Committee on Women in Industry*, argued that the principle of determining wages by family obligations should be rejected. At the same time the majority of the trade union movement was opposed to such ideas, seeing them as both an attack on their bargaining power and a dangerous alternative to their demand for a guaranteed weekly wage.

In fact both Beatrice Webb's and the trade union's objections were not to the concept of family endowment and the principle that it embodied, that women's place was in the home, but to the idea that it should be reckoned as part of the wage. Once it was established that the allowances should be paid from the Exchequer and the bargaining power of the unions was safeguarded the majority of the Labour Party waived its opposition.

It was in 1945 that the weight of the Labour Party came down fully in favour of defining women within the confines of the family. For the post-war policies adopted by the Labour government included not only the proposal for child allowances but swallowed whole the main concepts of the Beveridge Report on the position of women in society. William Beveridge, unlike the Labour Party, was not in two minds about the role of women. He stated quite categorically that the place of women was in the home. And the Labour Party in government, in implementing his ideas, for the first time took a clear stand. The Labour Party's 1945 election manifesto *Let us Face the Future* had prepared the ground for this move by echoing the main themes of the Beveridge Report:

> Labour will work especially for the care of British mothers and their children — children's allowances and school medical and feeding services, better maternity and child welfare services. A healthy family life must be fully ensured and parenthood must not be

penalised if the population of Britain is to be prevented from dwindling.[18]

In the actual report, *Social Insurance and Allied Services*, William Beveridge outlined a number of strict principles about the role of women in society and on them he built the entire structure of welfare state provisions. Despite the fact that at the time he was writing the report most working class women were engaged in the war industry, his two major principles were, first that 'during marriage most women will not be gainfully employed'; and secondly that, 'maternity is the main object of marriage'.[19] From these he proposed that the work of women in servicing this and the next generation of workers be recognised as an important social task:

> . . . the Plan for social security puts a premium on marriage in place of penalising it. . . . In the next thirty years housewives as mothers have vital work to do in ensuring the continuance of the British race and of British ideals in the world.[20]

By enmeshing the role of women in the home within a network of pension and social security schemes, tax and family allowances, William Beveridge made it extremely difficult for them to avoid this destiny.

The Beveridge Report, then, represented the beginnings of the pursuit of a definite family policy – a policy that was based primarily on the growing need in industry, after the technological advances made in production, for a skilled and well educated work force. As Margaret Wynn echoed in her book entitled *Family Policy*, 'It is accepted that the further advance of society depends on their being a large minority of quite highly educated people and upon the steady growth of this minority'.[21]

The Labour Party both in supporting William Beveridge's proposals and the education proposals that followed and largely complemented them, threw in its lot with this policy – a policy which rested on 'a partnership between parents and school to rear and mould the next generation'.[22] Accordingly, all the major education reports subsequent to 1945, Robbins, Crowther, Newsom and Plowden, stressed the importance of attuning education to the needs of industry and on defining its relationship to the family. The Newsom Report of 1963 remarked: 'We . . . think it essential to state at the outset the economic argument for investment in our pupils. The need is . . . for a generally better educated and intelligently adaptable labour force to meet new demands.'[23] Similarly, the Plowden Report of 1966 announced: 'It has been recognised that education is concerned with the whole man; henceforth it must be concerned with the whole family.'[24]

However, while it was accepted that education should take the form of this partnership, it was not accepted that this should mean that the woman's responsibility in child rearing should be in any way diminished. Indeed when the Plowden Report on nursery schools recommended their extension it was specifically stated that such a proposal should not be taken advantage of by woman who might choose to work: 'Low priority should be given to full-time nursery education for children whose mothers cannot satisfy the authorities that they have exceptionally good reasons for working.'[25]

John Bowlby's ideas on 'maternal deprivation'[26] were given great attention and indeed his conclusions were quoted by the Plowden Report to substantiate its findings. In fact John Bowlby's rather hysterical work on the dangers of 'maternal deprivation' reflected in an oblique way a real inconsistency in the government's family policy. That is, in the period of the implementation of the Beveridge Report and the various education policies there had actually been a sizeable increase in the number of women in employment. For while this emphasis on the socialisation and education of children was in tune with one of the major requirements of capital it was not with another. It failed to recognise that women had been drawn into the new jobs opening up in industry and that now they played an important role in this area of the economy as well as within the home as housewives.

In an important contribution outlining this problem,

Women's Two Roles – Home and Work, Alva Myrdal and Viola Klein, urged that government policy should be reshaped to reflect this fact. They revealed that at any given point in time three-quarters of all adult women were free from actual occupation with children. They considered this a waste of resources given the fact that industry was still at that time in need of an increased work-force. They warned that 'our modern economy cannot afford, nor can our democratic ideology tolerate, the existence of a large section of the population living by the efforts of others'.[27]

So instead of family policy assuming that women should completely orientate their lives around the home, Alva Myrdal and Viola Klein argued that it should address itself to a new problem:

> What are the working conditions most conducive to maximum efficiency, considering the fact that workers have responsibilities as well as jobs and that married women, in particular, often have arduous as well as important responsibilities at home.[28]

Their own answer to the problem was to extend Beveridge's original definition of women's role in society. They envisaged it in these terms,

> as a succession of three phases, each dominated mainly by one function: a period of training and education, followed, if possible, by years devoted to raising a family: these, in turn, being succeeded by a period during which past training and experience are put to wider social use.[29]

The beauty of this schema was that it made efficient use of women in the workforce while disrupting as little as possible the cultural and social norms of femininity in capitalist society. Women could take as their example, as Alva Myrdal and Viola Klein did in their book, that of Florence Horsburgh, once Minister of Education, who is reported as having said: 'I have had more satisfaction out of making a good steamed pudding than in any speech I have ever made in the House of Commons.'[30]

But the Labour Party displayed its customary indecision on

the position of women when faced with the need to amend the outlook embodied in the Beveridge Report. The contradictory pressures within the Labour Party in effect paralysed it and led it to ignore the recommendations and warnings of Myrdal and Klein. However, in the 1960s it came under mounting pressure to resolve this crisis in its policy. This pressure came simultaneously from three directions.

Firstly, there was systematic lobbying of the Labour government mounted under the leadership of Nancy Seear. In an article in *New Society*, 'Woman Power Needs a Policy', she returned to the main themes of Myrdal and Klein: 'Since married women form the main reserves and the shortage of labour is likely to continue, the importance of women in the total manpower budget needs no further emphasis.'[31] But she introduced at the same time a new and important point, namely that there was a danger that the most recent phases of the technological revolution in industry would have a catastrophic effect on the position of women within the workforce. In a paper for the Royal Commission on Trade Union and Employers' Associations she pointed out that: 'The jobs women are employed in are also those most likely to be modified or eliminated by technical change, and it is necessary to prepare them for less routine work.'[32]

The second pressure on the Labour government in the late 1960s was the necessities of meeting the requirements for joining the European Economic Community. Convention 100 of the Treaty of Rome spoke of equal pay for work of equal value, while Convention 111 of the International Labour Organisation went one step further and took up the issue of discrimination in respect of employment and occupation. Accordingly, if the Labour government was even to be in a position to become a member of the EEC it had to prepare legislation on the position of women on both these fronts.

But the third pressure was the most portentous. That was the upsurge of activity amongst women themselves. In June 1968 women sewing machinists at Ford's Dagenham plant went on strike over the question of grading. While the dispute was actually on the issue of job evalution it was reported in the press and generally publicised as on the issue of equal pay. Following the dispute a campaign on the joint issues of equal pay and equal rights for women quickly gained momentum. And out of this campaign emerged a new wave of feminism, the formation of the Women's Liberation Movement.

Under these three pressures the Labour government moved, but hesitantly and grudgingly. Although the Labour Party's 1964 election manifesto included the issue of equal pay, in 1966 Mr Gunter, the Minister of Labour, was still able to remark, 'it has been highlighted that none of us is sure what is meant by equal pay for equal work';[33] and in the following year he blamed both sides of industry for failing to 'tell us what they mean by equal pay'.[34]

It was not until 1975 and 1976 respectively, that the Labour government implemented its acts on equal pay and sex discrimination. By then, however, their arrival was most inopportune. For by this time British capitalism was clearly in the grips of a major economic and social crisis. And the Labour Party's response to this crisis had precipitated the threatened structural crisis in the position of women in society into a living reality. Nancy Seear's advice about training women for specific tasks in industry, which had in many ways been embodied in the equal pay and sex discrimination legislation, became dangerously outdated in the face of widespread unemployment and cuts in government spending. For her advice depended on sufficient resources for retraining facilities and an ability to plan and direct employment, both of which the Labour government considered out of the question in the mid 1970s. Indeed it was then looking in all directions for ways to cut its spending.

In order to do this the Labour government cut the budget of the welfare state. What followed in many cases was an unplanned running down of its services. The Health Service began to lean more heavily on the position of women in the home. Patients were sent home earlier and the mental hospitals released their populations on to an unprepared community. The extension of nursery schools was halted as local councils used the money allocated for it in other areas. Women were trapped in a pincer-like process. From the one side this reduction in welfare state services exacerbated their position within the family, where they were called upon to shoulder more and more of the burden of the reproduction of labour power. From the other side, their employment within welfare state service, such as teaching and social work, became threatened.

This threat of unemployment hit the whole range of 'women's work'. It has been estimated that in 1976 the rate of increase in female unemployment was three times the male rate. For example, part-time working, an area in which married women have traditionally been employed, was frequently scrapped when short-time working has been introduced into industry. And although many employers were able to avoid any detrimental effects on their wage bill from the Equal Pay Act in the five years they were given for its implementation, women workers were no longer such an attractive source of new labour.

Given its commitment to running a capitalist economy, the Labour government was unable to prevent most aspects of the social and economic crisis. However, its particular inabilities to formulate a clear policy to meet the changes in the position of women was a major contributive factor to this dimension of the crisis. As a working class party in some respects it attempted to pose as a champion of women's rights. But in practice it never succeeded. The 1967 Abortion legislation was introduced by private members and not by the Labour government. And in 1976 when restrictions were proposed to that legislation, it attempted to steer a course between the pro- and anti-abortionists. But when pushed it came down in favour of the latter.

The most important determinant of Labour Party policy on women remains the commitment it made in 1945 to the ideas of the Beveridge Report. And that commitment ties its hands in most directions, because to define the position of women in terms other than the confines of family life would entail the whole restructuring of welfare state provisions. For as we have seen, William Beveridge constructed them on that foundation. And as the proud architects of the welfare state in the days when their other claims to fame have become rather tarnished, the Labour government is unwilling to take on this task of demolition and reconstruction.

The fate of the Finer Report (1974) is a good indication of this. The Finer Report proposed a system of finance to one parent families separate from the existing Social Security benefits and which allowed a measure of choice to the person concerned whether or not to go out to work. However, to give this choice to people who in the majority of cases would be women is incompatible to the founding principle of the Beveridgean welfare state. So although the Finer Report has received a favourable response from the rank and file of the Labour Party in particular, it was shelved by its leadership. And that shelving was not simply because of a shortage of finance.

But in aggravating the structural crisis in the position of women, the Labour government plays a dangerous game. For that crisis gives a continuing impetus to the development of the women's movement. Like its predecessor, today's feminist movement in general has a suspicious attitude to the ideas of the Labour Party. But unlike that predecessor, it has at the same time developed and maintained links with the rest of the working class movement. The present campaign over abortion initiated by the women's movement gives every indication that the relationship between the feminist and labour movement will not be a repeat of the barren one in the days of the suffragettes.

The present feminist movement differs from that at the turn of the century in another important respect. Unlike the suffragettes, today's feminists have considered the question of developing an analysis of their oppression an important aspect of their practical activity. And from that analysis the beginnings of strategy has begun to emerge which is not, like the suffragettes', limited to one issue but aims at a radical restructuring of all relations in society. A strategy that is based on an understanding of both the class antagonisms in society and the importance of the sexual relations between men and women. A strategy that is beginning to learn from both the strengths and weaknesses of Marx and Freud.

14.
Feminism and revolution

An index of the extent that revolutionary thought has broken from the limitations of its liberal heritage is the degree to which an understanding of women's oppression is integral to it. As we have seen, the ideas of freedom and women's liberation were opposed in liberal thought in the nineteenth century. The political framework of liberalism which dominated radical thought up to the time of Marx rested on the separation of the public sphere from the private, industry from the family. Thus, despite the writings of John Stuart Mill and Mary Wollstonecraft, in reality the freedom of the man in the first sphere took its meaning from the restriction of women to the second. But within revolutionary thought in the twentieth century the ideas of freedom and women's liberation remained separated. Although Marx and Engels developed a historical account of the oppression of women they left incomplete the analysis of the strategic relation between the struggle for women's liberation and the proletarian revolution. What then are the necessary steps in spelling out that relation?

The first step was provided indirectly by the writings of Freud. His uneasy liberalism highlighted the neglect of the sexual aspect of the oppression in the relations of men to women that was a feature common to both radical and revolutionary thought. Jean-Paul Sartre and Simone de Beauvoir helped to develop the argument a little further through the importance they gave to the failure of the sexual relation between men and women by its disintegration into the forms of subjectivity and alterity. The man defines himself against the woman, but in reducing her to an object he in turn fails to confirm his humanity. But the decisive step was to establish the centrality of women's oppression to the basic relations of capitalism, that is to extend the marxist concept of alienation to explain this relationship of subjectivity and alterity between men and women. While alienation reduces the man to an instrument of labour within industry, it reduces the woman to an instrument for his sexual pleasure within the family. In this way the defining of femininity in capitalist society becomes a key aspect of the alienated form which productive activity takes within the relations of commodity production. Accordingly, a challenge to the position of women in society must be integral to a revolutionary assault on the capitalist system. But while this gives a theoretical answer to the problem of the relationship between women's oppression and class oppression, what form in practice should the struggle take? And, in particular, what should be the relation of the working class to the feminist movement?

Traditionally the marxist movement has attempted to reduce the second to the first and has been very wary of the autonomy of the women's movement. This immediately causes problems because the present women's movement has its origins and roots firmly in its autonomous groups – the consciousness-raising groups. It was in these women-only groups that women began to look at themselves through their own eyes rather than through those of men. In other words, it was here that women started the often painful process of breaking through the experience of femininity. By discussing and comparing their individual experiences women developed an understanding of the emotional structures of their dependency. They became aware that their individual problems were simultaneously political problems – that their position as the Other in society was the historical product of a capitalist society. And so, through collective discussion, women were able to move beyond the experience of the reification of interpersonal relations. For the discussion of emotional and sexual feelings in political terms gradually divested them of their character of being the most immediate, and therefore most natural ones in society.

But the consciousness-raising groups did not of themselves provide women with a political practice. As women attempted to define themselves as autonomous individuals, independent of their relations with men, a tendency arose towards introversion. Some women began to suggest that the way to break finally with the experience of femininity and its structures of emotional dependency was to sever all relations with men. For them the women's movement itself became both the beginning and the end of the struggle for liberation. Accordingly, the autonomy of the women's movement began to be interpreted by some feminists as the path of separatism – the separation of women from all areas of life that were dominated by men.

These discussions on the form of the women's movement cannot, however, be divorced from the problem of its composition. As we have seen, it was the growing contradictions in the feminine stereotype together with a structural crisis in the position of women in society which gave the impetus to the growth of the women's movement in advanced capitalism – a process which affects both working class and middle class women. And yet the women who were first attracted to the women's movement and on the whole who continue to dominate it, are young, middle class and well educated. This can be partially explained by the fact that the initial experience of this contradiction is different for middle class and working class women. Middle class women experienced it as a conflict between the traditions of femininity and their aspirations and abilities. At the same time, particularly if they were young and unmarried, they were relatively free to explore the contradictions in the position of women. But for working class women who were tied in strong material ways to their families this did not appear an attractive prospect, especially as working class culture has always been more hostile to individual deviation than middle class culture. Not that there has been no response by working class women to the growing contradictions in their situation. In Britain in the last few years struggles (over equal pay and job discrimination) have been initiated largely by working class women – a factor of particular significance given that these struggles continued during a period when the rest of their class was relatively passive.

It appeared, then, that feminists were faced with a choice – either to continue discussing within the consciousness-raising groups, or, if they wanted to make contact with working class women and extend the reach of the women's movement, to abandon them in favour of campaigning bodies. In Britain many feminists made their decision by throwing their energies into the abortion campaign, but a significant number of them became rapidly disaffected. While they recognised that the fight for freely available abortion, like that over equal pay or opportunities, was necessary if women were to achieve any real degree of freedom, they felt nevertheless that something was lacking. These demands seemed detached from the experience that they had begun to release in the consciousness-raising groups. It appeared that activity around these issues could skate quite happily over the really oppressive structures of femininity. Approached as formal demands they seemed little advance on the well-worn formulas that the left had always returned to when attempting to deal with the women's question. And on top of this their presence as feminists within the campaign was overshadowed by that of the organised left.

So were women to conclude from this experience that there are no forms of activity open to the women's movement that could reveal the totality of women's oppression? In other words that feminists are faced with the inevitable dilemma of choosing between the traditional perspective of the left or that of the separatists – of raising a series of formal demands and pledging faith in the ultimate victory of the proletarian revolution or allowing the women's movement to turn in on itself in a spiral of introversion? When we look a little more closely, however, the problem of the political perspective of the women's movement is seen to be at the same time a problem of the traditional definition of politics.

While revolutionary marxists broke from the domination of liberalism over political thought with their conclusion that human freedom could not in reality be achieved by reforming society but only through the process of revolution, they still accepted to a certain extent the liberal definition of what were political matters and what were not. On the whole they considered that their own subjective experience, their own individual relations, were not of political concern. To put it another way, the old liberal separation of the public from the private, the political from the personal, found a new home within the practice of the left. In recent times for women whose radicalisation has taken place primarily in the women's movement this had led to a particularly intolerable form of oppression. Its most crude forms were the relegating of women to typing and tea-making roles within the organisations of the left, and generally servicing male revolutionaries' needs. But its less obvious forms were (and are) in many ways more insidious. By failing to consider personal interaction a political question, the forms of organisation and discussion that the left groups adopted both internally and in the campaigns that they initiated prevented the full participation of women. The aggressive and often destructive approach of men to political debate reflects their traditional ability to distance themselves from their political practice. Historically the political and personal lives of men have been structurally separate. Unlike women, their involvement in politics has not required them to question their very individuality. The left groups, in their lack of sensitivity to personal interaction, reproduced a traditionally male approach to politics and with it an effective exclusion of women from real political involvement.

But, as we have seen, the perpetuation of this separation of public from private life is not limited to the practice of the revolutionary left groups – it is a general and restricting feature of political life in advanced capitalist countries. In Britain Labour governments have shied away from recognising issues which relate directly to family life as political. The legislation they have passed has assumed the framework of the Beveridge Report of 1942 – the defining of women in terms of the family. Given this assumption Labour governments have maintained the role of women as wives and mothers to be above political interference. When faced with an issue that threatens that definition, such as the availability of abortion, they have attempted to side-step the problem by referring to it as a matter of 'individual conscience'. The trade union movement also maintains this separation in its own way by drawing a line between industry and the family. Although the issues of abortion and childcare facilities are of crucial importance to its women members the trade union movement has classed them as outside its scope of activity. For the tradition of the trade unions rests on taking action only on those issues which arise directly from their members' conditions of work, and more specifically, male members' conditions of work. Since the beginning of the seventies women trade unionists, primarily in white collar sectors, have chalked up some success in getting their unions to take a stand on such issues as abortion or childcare facilities. But while this is an encouraging trend the weight of tradition particularly in the strongest and longest organised sections of the working class remains a block to their actions.

This defining of political activity in terms of the separation of industry from the family obviously limits the effectiveness of working class struggle by exacerbating the divisions within it on the basis of sex. Moreover, by reinforcing the experience of alienation and reification on which it is based it puts a brake on the development of revolutionary consciousness within the working class. For the development of such a consciousness is dependent on the working class being able to grasp the reality of capitalist society beyond the level at which it immediately presents itself. In other words it must begin to understand the experience of reification and alienation in order to break through the opacity of bourgeois ideology.

It is here that the intervention of the women's movement could be the crucial factor, for by experiencing the separation of industry from the family most acutely women can be the most effective agent of breaking down this separation in all its forms. This, then, simultaneously begins to resolve the problem of the political perspective of the women's movement and adds a new dimension to political struggle.

Firstly, the women's movement can help transform the traditionally limited location of political struggle. When sections of the working class take up an issue, feminists can fight for its extension beyond simply the trade union or Labour Party constituency. They can argue rather that it should take in the women's movement itself, the housing estates, the student unions and so on.

Secondly, the women's movement can transform the traditional content of political struggle. Obviously, as its first step, it will have to convince the working class movement of the importance of taking up campaigns that strike at the material aspects of women's oppression, such as abortion, contraception and adequate nursery facilities. But at the same time it can use these campaigns as a starting point for questioning the polarity of masculinity and femininity in capitalist society. So, for example, the present abortion campaign has hit at the idea that sex is just for procreation. However, in raising the question of women's control over their fertility and sexuality it can also go on to question the inevitability of genital sexuality and male-female relationships. That is, while starting with a formal political demand feminists can, in the course of a campaign, challenge the normal limitations of political concern.

Thirdly, the women's movement can transform the traditional form of political struggle. Here the question of autonomy becomes all important. For by maintaining the importance of self-organisation feminists can immediately turn the form of the organisation of campaigns into a political issue. They can do this by fighting for the establishment of women's caucuses in all areas of political life, from the traditional working class organisations to the campaigns of the revolutionary left. In this way the question of autonomy can be used to extend the boundaries of the women's movement rather than turning it in on itself – to begin to solve the problem of its limited middle class composition. In joining together, women can gain the strength to fight in those organisations to which they already belong rather than separating themselves off from them. For working class women it provides the opportunity for them to establish independently their own form of response to oppression without it being imposed upon them by the women who at present make up the women's movement. Self-organisation, then, enables working class and middle class women to come together in the women's movement on a political basis, each from their own sense of strength. This sensitivity to individual experience can in turn be applied to the forms of political discussion. Perhaps gradually small workshop discussions, a feature of the women's movement which allows the individual to contribute and recognises the validity of his or her personal experience, could replace more formal types of debate. In short, the organised presence of women could prevent the traditional exclusion of women in both its crude and more sophisticated forms. And by asserting the right of women to define their own identity within political structures, the self-organisation of women strikes at the heart of the feminine attitude of alterity on which this exclusion rests. Ultimately, then, autonomy provides a political and not simply an organisational link between the feminist and the working class struggle.

Revolutionary marxists have argued that the question of self-organisation is decisive to the development of revolutionary consciousness within the working class. They have considered the development of soviety-type bodies, which oppose the decision-making powers of the working class to those of the bourgeois state, as the most important form of political struggle. Marx laid the basis for this point when he argued that revolutionary consciousness depended on the working class becoming a class for itself: that is, through recognising its position within society at the same time it realises its historical task as the agent for social change. The women's movement through its very development and form of organisation expresses most clearly the need for this self-conscious attitude to political struggle and can thereby ensure that the transformation of the working class into a class for itself takes place at the highest political level.

References

Place of publication is London, or Harmondsworth in the case of Penguin books, unless otherwise indicated.

Chapter 1 / pp.9–12

1. Quoted from *Punch* in C.Rover, *Women's Suffrage and Party Politics in Britain 1866–1914*, Routledge and Kegan Paul 1974, p.127.
2. M.Wollstonecraft, *A Vindication of the Rights of Women*, Everyman's Library, J.M.Dent 1965, p.11.
3. J.S.Mill, *The Subjection of Women*, Everyman's Library, J.M.Dent 1965, p.237.
4. *ibid.* p.265.
5. *Révolution de Paris* quoted in C.Tomalin, *The Life and Death of Mary Wollstonecraft*, Weidenfeld and Nicolson 1974, p.155.
6. Quoted in A.Rosen, *Rise Up, Women!*, Routledge and Kegan Paul 1974, p.10.

Chapter 2 / pp.13–24

1. S.Freud, 'The Sexual Life of Human Beings' (1917), *Introductory Lectures on Psychoanalysis*, Pelican Books 1974, p.361.
2. See in particular K.Millett, *Sexual Politics*, Abacus 1972 and S. de Beauvoir, *The Second Sex*, Penguin Books 1972.
3. See J.Mitchell, *Psychoanalysis and Feminism*, Pelican Books 1975.
4. S.Freud, 'Femininity' (1933), *New Introductory Lectures on Psychoanalysis*, Pelican Books 1975, p.148.
5. *ibid.* p.160.

6. See J.Mitchell, *op. cit.* pp.42–52.

7. M.Bonaparte, *Female Sexuality*, New York: Evergreen Edition, Grove Press 1962, p.8.

8. *ibid.* p.1.

9. S.Freud, 'Totem and Taboo' (1913), in J.Strachey (ed), *The Standard Edition of the Complete Psychological Works of Sigmund Freud*, vol.XXI, Hogarth Press 1961, p.142.

10. E.Reed, *Women's Evolution*, New York: Pathfinder Press 1975, p.341.

11. M.Mead, *Male and Female*, Gollancz 1950, p.191.

12. E.Reed, *op. cit.* p.343.

13. A.Oakley, *Sex, Gender and Society*, Maurice Temple Smith 1972, p.120.

14. C. Lévi-Strauss, 'The Family', in H.C.Shapiro (ed), *Man, Culture and Society*, New York: Galaxy Books, OUP 1956, p.345.

15. M.Mead, *op. cit.* p.152.

16. G.N.Garmonsway (ed), *The Penguin English Dictionary*, Penguin Books 1965.

17. J.Goody, 'Incest and Adultery', in J.Goody (ed), *Kinship*, Penguin Books 1971.

18. See particularly S.Freud, 'Beyond the Pleasure Principle' (1921), in J.Strachey (ed), *The Standard Edition of the Complete Psychological Works of Sigmund Freud*, vol.XVIII, Hogarth Press 1957; and his other major texts after 1921.

19. S.Freud, 'The Group Psychology and the Analysis of the Ego' (1921), in *ibid.*

Chapter 3 / pp.25–29

1. K.Marx, *Economic and Philosophic Manuscripts of 1844*, Lawrence and Wishart 1968, p.137, emphasis in the original.

2. F.Engels, 'Origin of the Family, Private Property and the State', in *Marx and Engels Selected Works*, Lawrence and Wishart 1968, p.488.

3. *ibid.* p.484.

4. *ibid.* p.507.

5. *ibid.* p.499.

6. K.Marx, *The German Ideology*, Lawrence and Wishart 1968, p.192.

7. F.Engels, *op. cit.* p.495.

Chapter 4 / pp.30–41

1. K.Marx, 'Critique of the Gotha Programme', *Marx and Engels Selected Works*, Lawrence and Wishart 1968, p.330.
2. F.Engels, 'The Origin of the Family, Private Property and the State', in *ibid.* p.50.
3. Quoted in L.Colletti, *From Rousseau to Lenin*, New Left Books 1972, p.68.
4. Quoted in G.Lichtheim, *Marxism. An Historical and Critical Study*, Routledge and Kegan Paul 1961, p.298.
5. G.Plekhanov, *Selected Philosophical Works*, vol.1, Lawrence and Wishart 1961, p.734.
6. Quoted in Preface to G.Plekhanov, *op. cit.* p.43.
7. A.Bebel, *Women under Socialism*, New York: Schocken Books 1971, p.180.
8. Quoted in W.Thönnessen, *The Emancipation of Women. The Rise and Decline of the Women's Movement in German Social Democracy 1863–1933*, Pluto Press 1973, p.136.
9. L.Trotsky, *The Revolution Betrayed*, New Park Publications 1973, p.144, emphasis added.
10. A.Kollontai, *Sexual Relations and the Class Struggle*, Bristol: Falling Wall Press 1972, pp.3–4.
11. S.Rowbotham, *Women, Resistance and Revolution*, Penguin 1972, p.162.

Chapter 5 / pp.42–63

1. W.Reich, *Dialectical Materialism and Psychoanalysis*, Socialist Reproduction 1972, p.53.
2. J.Mitchell, *Psychoanalysis and Feminism*, Pelican Books 1975, p.412.
3. From 'Beyond the Pleasure Principle' (1921) onwards.
4. S.Freud, 'The Paths to the Formation of Symptoms' (1917), *Introductory Lectures on Psychoanalysis*, Pelican Books 1974, p.422, emphasis in the original.
5. S.Freud, *The Ego and the Id* (1923), Hogarth Press 1962, p.35.
6. *ibid.* p.26.
7. S.Freud, 'Beyond the Pleasure Principle' (1921), in J.Strachey (ed),

The Standard Edition of the Complete Psychological Works of Sigmund Freud, vol.XVIII, Hogarth Press 1957, p.42.

8. J.Mitchell, *op. cit.* p.415.

9. *ibid.* p.413.

10. *ibid.* p.369.

11. W.Reich, *The Sexual Revolution*, Vision Press 1972, p.16.

12. W.Reich, *Dialectical Materialism and Psychoanalysis*, Socialist Reproduction 1972, p.25.

13. W.Reich, *The Mass Psychology of Fascism*, Pelican Books 1975, p.39.

14. *ibid.* p.138.

15. H.Marcuse, *Eros and Civilization*, Abacus 1972, p.42.

16. *ibid.* p.145.

17. S.Freud, *op. cit.* p.57.

18. H.Marcuse, *op. cit.* p.115.

19. *ibid.* p.81.

20. S.Freud, 'Civilization and its Discontents' (1929), in J.Strachey (ed), *The Standard Edition of the Complete Psychological Works of Sigmund Freud*, Hogarth Press 1961, vol.XXI, p.134.

21. H.Marcuse, *op. cit.* p.78.

22. *ibid.*

23. S.Freud, 'Instincts and Their Vicissitudes' (1915), in J.Strachey (ed), *Collected Papers of Sigmund Freud*, vol.IV, Hogarth Press 1925, p.65, emphasis added.

24. K.Marx, *Economic and Philosophical Manuscripts of 1844*, Lawrence and Wishart 1968, p.113.

25. S.Freud, 'Group Psychology and the Analysis of the Ego' (1921), in J.Strachey (ed), *The Standard Edition of the Complete Psychological Works of Sigmund Freud*, vol.XVIII, Hogarth Press 1957, p.79.

Chapter 6 / pp.64–69

1. K.Marx, *Capital*, vol.1, Lawrence and Wishart 1970, p.73.

2. K.Marx, *Economic and Philosophical Manuscripts of 1844*, Lawrence and Wishart 1973, p.156.

3. S.Freud, 'Civilization and its Discontents', in J.Strachey (ed), *The Standard Edition of the Complete Psychological Works of Sigmund Freud*, vol.XXI, Hogarth Press 1961, p.77.

4. *ibid*. pp.77–79.

5. *ibid*. p.95.

6. K.Marx, *On the Jewish Question*, Blackwell 1971, p.235.

7. S.Freud, *op. cit*. p.111.

Chapter 7/ pp.70–78

1. K.Marx, *Grundrisse*, edited by D.McLellan, Macmillan 1971, p.66.

2. G.Lukacs, *History and Class Consciousness*, Merlin Press 1971, p.184.

3. *ibid*.

4. *ibid*. p.178.

5. *ibid*. p.58.

6. *ibid*. p.62.

7. K.Marx, *Economic and Philosophical Manuscripts of 1844*, Lawrence and Wishart 1973, p.110.

8. K.Marx, *Grundrisse*, edited by D.McLellan, Macmillan 1971, p.70.

9. M.Mead, *Male and Female*, Gollancz 1950, p.371.

10. T.Parsons and R.F.Bales, *The Family, Socialization and Interaction Process*, Routledge and Kegan Paul 1956, pp.21–22.

11. A.Oakley, *The Sociology of Housework*, Martin Robertson 1974, p.28.

Chapter 8 / pp.79–86

1. Abridged and translated version of J.-P.Sartre, 'Questions of method', in D.G.Cooper and R.D.Laing, *Reason and Violence*, Tavistock Publications 1964, p.39.

2. J.-P.Sartre, *Being and Nothingness*, University Paperback, Methuen & Co. Ltd 1972, p. 383.

3. K.Marx, *Economic and Philosophical Manuscripts of 1844*, Lawrence and Wishart 1973, p.182.

4. J.-P.Sartre, *op. cit*. p. 393.

5. *ibid*. p.391.

6. *ibid*. p.398.

7. *ibid*. p.363.

8. *ibid*. p.408.

9. S. de Beauvoir, *The Second Sex*, Penguin Books 1972, p.15.

10. *ibid*. p.18.
11. *ibid*. p.406.
12. *ibid*. p.427.
13. *ibid*. p.443.

Chapter 9 / pp.87–92

1. A.Clarke, *The Working Life of Women in the Seventeenth Century*, Routledge 1919, p.35.
2. Quoted I.Watt, *The Rise of the Novel*, Pelican Books 1972, p.161.
3. *op. cit*.
4. F.Engels, *The Conditions of the Working Class in England*, Panther Books 1974, p.248.

Chapter 10 / pp.93–99

1. Quoted by I.Watt, *The Rise of the Novel*, Pelican Books 1972, p.183.
2. *ibid*.
3. *ibid*. p.191.
4. *ibid*. p.171.

Chapter 11 / pp.100–111

1. J.Berger, *Ways of Seeing*, British Broadcasting and Penguin Books 1973, p.47.

Chapter 12 / pp.112–130

1. M.Benston, 'The Political Economy of Women's Liberation', *Monthly Review*, vol.21, no.4.
2. M.Dalla Costa, *The Power of Women and the Subversion of the Community*, Bristol: Falling Wall Press 1973, p.31, p.52.
3. M.Coulson, B.Magas, H.Wainwright, 'The Housewife and her Labour under Capitalism – A Critique', *New Left Review*, no.89, p.60.
4. W.Seccombe, 'The Housewife and her Labour under Capitalism', *New Left Review*, no.83, reprinted in *Red Pamphlet* no.8, p.8.
5. *ibid*. p.9.

6. J.Gardiner, 'Women's Domestic Labour', *New Left Review*, no.89, p.50.

7. *ibid.* p.50.

8. W.Seccombe, *op. cit.* p.16.

9. K.Marx, *Grundrisse*, edited by M.Nicolaus, Pelican Books 1973, p.533.

10. *ibid.*

11. *ibid.* p.532.

12. *ibid.*

13. F.Engels, 'The Origin of the Family, Private Property and the State', *Marx and Engels Selected Works*, Lawrence and Wishart 1968, p.569.

14. K.Marx, *Capital*, vol.1, Lawrence and Wishart 1970, p.395.

15. W.Seccombe, *op. cit.* p.6.

16. K.Marx, 'Wages, Price and Profit', *Marx and Engels Selected Works*, Lawrence and Wishart 1968, p.222.

17. Quoted by M.Ramelson, *The Petticoat Rebellion*, Lawrence and Wishart 1967, p.103.

18. K.Marx, 'Wages, Price and Profit', *op. cit.* p.222.

19. K.Marx, *Grundrisse*, edited by M.Nicolaus, Pelican Books 1973, p.531.

20. *ibid.* p.101.

21. K.Marx, 'Wages, Price and Profit', *op. cit.* p.208.

22. M.Benston, *op. cit.*

23. M.Coulson, B.Magas, H.Wainwright, *op. cit.* pp.61, 68.

24. *ibid.* p.69.

25. J.Gardiner, *op. cit.* p.56.

Chpater 13 / pp.131–149

1. T.Nairn, 'The Fateful Meridian', *New Left Review*, no.60.

2. *ibid.* pp.32–33.

3. *ibid.*

4. S.Rowbotham, *Hidden from History*, Pluto Press 1973, p.60.

5. 'Women in Society – Women at Work', *The Listener*, 7 November 1974, vol.92.

6. A.Rosen, *Rise Up, Women!*, Routledge and Kegan Paul 1974, p.66.

7. C.Rover, *Women's Suffrage and Party Politics in Britain 1866–1914*, Routledge and Kegan Paul 1967, p.14.

8. Quoted by A.Rosen, *op. cit.* p.96.

9. *ibid.* p.183.

10. Quoted *ibid.* p.218.

11. Quoted *ibid.* p.250.

12. T.Nairn, *op. cit.* p.4.

13. In Dr M.Philips (ed), *Women and the Labour Party*, Headly Bros. 1919, p.14.

14. *ibid.* p.33.

15. *ibid.* p.47.

16. E.R.Rathbone, *The Ethics and Economics of Family Endowment*, The Epworth Press 1927, p.9.

17. *ibid.* p.12.

18. Labour Party Manifesto 1945, *Let Us Face the Future*, p.10.

19. 'Social Insurance and Allied Services', *Parliamentary Paper*, HMSO, reprinted 1968, p.50.

20. *ibid.* p.52, p.53.

21. M.Wynn, *Family Policy*, Michael Joseph 1970, p.240.

22. *ibid.* p.25.

23. Quoted in *ibid.* p.25.

24. *ibid.*

25. 'Children and their Primary Schools, a Report of the Central Advisory Council for Education', vol.1, *Parliamentary Papers*, HMSO 1966.

26. J.Bowlby, 'Maternal Care and Mental Health', World Health Organisation Monograph Geneva. And see L. Comer's critique in *The Myth of Motherhood*, Spokesman Pamphlet no.21, Nottingham n.d.

27. A.Myrdal and V.Klein, *Women's Two Roles – Home and Work*, Routledge and Kegan Paul 1956, p.26.

28. *ibid.* p.94.

29. *ibid.* p.142.

30. *ibid.* p.141.

31. *New Society* vol.1, no.9, 1962.

32. N.Seear, 'The Position of Women in Industry', *Royal Commission on Trade Unions and Employers' Associations*, Research Papers 11, 1968, p.1.

33. Quoted by P.Pinder, *Women at Work*, PEP 1969, p.528.

34. *ibid.* p.529.

Index